Danish Learner's Dictionary:

1001 Danish Words in Frequency Order with Example Sentences

KAMILA HELGER

OLIVER I. HENRIKSEN

CONTENTS

"One language sets you in a corridor for life. Two languages open every door along the way."
— Frank Smith

ACKNOWLEDGMENTS

I would like to express my sincere gratitude to everyone who contributed to the research, proofreading, editing and writing of this book, in particular writing and editing all of the example sentences.

Thank you.

ABBREVIATIONS

abb	abbreviation
adj	adjective
adv	adverb
art	article
conj	conjunction
int	interjection
nc	common gender noun
nn	neuter gender noun
npl	plural noun
num	numeral
part	particle
prep	preposition
pro	pronoun
v	verb

INTRODUCTION

What is a frequency dictionary?

A frequency dictionary is essentially a list of vocabulary words for a foreign language that is organized in order of how common the words are in the language, and not in alphabetical order as with traditional dictionaries.

The value of a frequency dictionary for students of a foreign language is to enable students to focus on the most common words in a language and thus ensure that the effort spent learning new vocabulary items is spent as efficiently as possible. Traditional foreign language textbooks typically present vocabulary in thematic lists, which can aid memorization but without any frequency information, students are unsure if they are memorizing words that they actually need or not. Learning from thematic lists also has the potential to leave gaps in the student's vocabulary for very frequent words that do not fit neatly into the thematic framework.

Frequency dictionaries such as this one are best used as a supplement to more traditional courses and dictionaries and are very useful tools to discover and memorize frequent words that the student has not yet mastered. However, this frequency dictionary does not teach Danish grammar or pronunciation and therefore should not be considered a standalone course to learn the Danish language.

Where do the words come from?

The word list used to create this dictionary was adapted from a larger list of the most common 5000 words from Danish subtitles available on opensubtitles.org. Consequently, the words selected largely represent content from movies and television and therefore are more in the spoken register of the language as opposed to a more literary register. It is our hope that using a corpus of subtitles will additionally expose the reader to the more colloquial and informal spoken language to balance the more literary content often presented to students in more traditional courses.

Additionally, because the content comes from movies and television shows, the list contains words that are not appropriate in all contents, including words considered swear words. The decision was made not to delete these words from the corpus. This was done in order to expose students to words that they will likely hear anyways, and to teach them to be aware of these words that could possibly offend. Any potentially inappropriate language is labeled as "vulgar" in its entry and students are advised to avoid using these words altogether. Although native speakers may use these words quite often, it is very hard for second language speakers to be able to tell how these vulgar words will be received and the potential to cause undue offence is too great.

Which word forms are included?

Words in the Danish language change forms based on various grammatical rules, as do words in many languages including English, and what word forms to include in a frequency list is a decision that must be made when compiling the list. To use an example from English, are 'ran' and 'run' the same word? What about 'am', 'are' and 'is'? The approach that has been taken in this book is as follows:

1. Regular verb forms that exactly follow the pattern of **lave: jeg laver, jeg lavede, jeg har lavet,** are only listed once under the normal dictionary form. This is the most common and most regular verb conjugation in Danish.
2. Irregular verb forms are listed separately as they occur in the frequency list. Although there are comparatively few irregular verbs in the Danish language, they number among the most frequently used verbs and therefore must be mastered in all their forms.
3. Definite nouns where **–en** or **–et** is added to the word are combined with the basic noun, e.g. **huset** "the house", is listed under **hus**.
4. Regular plurals that add either **–(e)r** or **–e** are combined with the singular forms. Irregular plurals are listed separately.
5. Names of people and places have all been removed.
6. Regular adjective forms that add **–t** in the neuter and **–e** in the plural have been combined with the common singular adjective. The neuter form is however listed separately if it is the adverb form.
7. Words that are spelled the same, but have two distinct meanings frequent enough to justify including both, are listed with their separate meanings as individual entries.
8. Onomatopoeia (ooh, ah, oww etc.) have all been removed.

Although the above philosophy has guided the selection of words, exceptions have occasionally been made if it was felt to benefit the reader.

INTRODUCTION

In the main frequency index of words, which accounts for the majority of this book, each vocabulary entry includes the basic part of speech, a simple English translation or translations, an example Danish sentence showing the word's correct usage, and an English translation of the example sentence.

To supplement the frequency index, a traditional alphabetical index of all 1001 words has been included at the back of this book. This can be used as a quick reference to find a specific word. The alphabetical index includes the part of speech, the basic English translation and its position in the frequency index for further reference.

FREQUENCY INDEX

1. **er** *v* is, am, are (present tense of **være**)
   - **Hvem er du?**
     Who are you?

2. **jeg** *pro* I
   - **Jeg er høj.**
     I am tall.

3. **det** *pro* that, it
   - **Det er godt.**
     It is good.

4. **det** *art* the (before neuter adjective)
   - **Det Hvide Hus**
     The White House

5. **du** *pro* you
   - **Hvem er du?**
     Who are you?

6. **i** *prep* in
   - **I Danmark de taler dansk.**
     In Denmark they speak Danish.

7. **ikke** *adv* not (negation)
   - **Jeg er ikke høj.**
     I am not tall.

8. **at** part to (infinitive marker)
   - **Rart at møde dig.**
     Pleased to meet you.

9. **en** *art* a, an (before common noun)
   - **Hav en god dag.**
   Have a good day.

10. **og** *conj* and
    - **Han har en kat og en hund.**
    He has a cat and a dog.

11. **har** *v* has (present tense of **have**)
    - **Jeg har en søster.**
    I have a sister.

12. **vi** *pro* we
    - **Vi er danske.**
    We are Danish.

13. **til** *adv* to, for, until
    - **Gå hen til huset.**
    Go to the house.

14. **på** *prep* on
    - **Det er på bordet.**
    It is on the table.

15 **hvad** *pro* what
    - **Hvad laver du?**
    What are you doing?

16 **mig** *pro* me
    - **Kom med mig.**
    Come with me.

17. **med** *prep* with
    - **Gå med hende.**
    Go with her.

18. **de** *art* the (before plural adjective), those
    - **De gule huse**
    The yellow houses

19. **de** *pro* they
- **De er svenske.**
  They are Swedish.

20. **den** *art* the (before common adjective), that
- **Den røde bil.**
  The red car.

21. **for** *prep* for, of, to
- **Det er på tide for mig at forlade.**
  It is time for me to leave.

22. **for** *adv* too
- **Nu er det for sent.**
  Now it is too late.

23. **der** *adv* there
- **Hvad er lige der?**
  What is right there?

24. **der** *pro* who, which (relative pronoun)
- **Jens, der er min ven, er en læge.**
  Jens, who is my friend, is a doctor.

25. **så** *v* saw (past tense of **se**)
- **I går så jeg hende.**
  Yesterday I saw her.

26. **så** *adv* so
- **Det er så koldt i dag.**
  It is so cold today.

27. **dig** *pro* you
- **Jeg elsker dig.**
  I love you.

28. **han** *pro* he
- **Han er syg.**
  He is sick.

29. **kan** *v* can, be able (present tense of **kunne**)
    - **Jeg kan ikke gå.**
      I cannot go.

30. **af** *prep*, adv   by, of, from, off
    - **Jeg hørte det af ham.**
      I heard it from him.

31. **vil** *v* want to, shall, will (present tense of **ville**)
    - **Jeg vil have noget at spise.**
      I want something to eat.

32. **var** *v* was (past tense of **være**)
    - **Hun var der ikke.**
      She wasn't there.

33. **her** *adv* here
    - **Hvem er her?**
      Who is here?

34. **et** *art* a, an (before neuter noun)
    - **Et blåt hus.**
      A blue house.

35. **skal** *v* will (future), shall, should (present tense of **skulle**)
    - **Jeg skal nok være der i morgen.**
      I will be there tomorrow.

36. **ved** *v* know (present tense of **vide**)
    - **Jeg ved ikke.**
      I don't know.

37. **men** *conj* but
    - **Han er rar, men doven.**
      He is nice, but lazy.

38. **om** *prep* about
    - **Vi taler om dig.**
      We are talking about you.

39. **nu** *adv* now
    - **Hvad er klokken nu?**
      What time is it now?

40. **som** *pro* who, which, that (relative pronoun)
    - **Jeg har en kæreste, som er smuk.**
      I have a girlfriend who is beautiful.

41. **ja** *int* yes
    - **Ja, jeg taler dansk.**
      Yes, I speak Danish.

42. **min** *pro* my
    - **Det er min hat.**
      That is my hat.

43. **nej** *int* no
    - **Nej, jeg kan ikke forstå dansk.**
      No, I can't understand Danish.

44. **noget** *pro* some, something (neuter form of **nogen**)
    - **Det er noget andet.**
      It is something else.

45. **ham** *pro* him
    - **Jeg kan lide ham.**
      I like him.

46. **hun** *pro* she
    - **Hun er højere end ham.**
      She is taller than him.

47. **være** *v* to be
    - **Jeg kan være din ven.**
      I can be your friend.

48. **bare** *adv* just, simply, only
    - **Bare gør det.**
      Just do it.

49. **kom** *v* came (imperative and past tense of **komme**)
- **Hvornår kom han?**
  When did he come?

50. **din** *pro* your, yours
- **Er det din mor?**
  Is this your mother?

51. **hvor** *adv* where
- **Hvor er restauranten?**
  Where is the restaurant?

52. **os** *pro* us
- **Giv det til os.**
  Give it to us.

53. **dem** *pro* them
- **Det er ikke for dem.**
  It is not for them.

54. **hvis** *conj* if
- **Hvis hun er syg, vil hun ikke komme.**
  If she's sick she won't come.

55. **ud** *adv* out
- **Kom ud af huset.**
  Get out of the house.

56. **må** *v* can, may, must (present tense of **måtte**)
- **Det må være koldt.**
  It must be cold.

57. **fra** *prep* from
- **Han kommer fra Island.**
  He comes from Iceland.

58. **se** *v* to see
- **Jeg vil ikke se hende nu.**
  I don't want to see her now.

59. **god** *adj* good
- **Hun er en god arbejder.**
  She is a good worker.

60. **have** *v* to have
- **Du kan ikke have det.**
  You can't have that.

61. **ville** *v* to want to, shall, will, should
- **Jeg vil besøge dig i morgen.**
  I will visit you tomorrow.

62. **gøre** *v* to do
- **Hvad vil du gøre?**
  What do you want to do?

63. **lige** *adj* straight, even, just
- **Luk lige døren.**
  Just go close the door.

64. **alle** *pro* all (plural of **al**)
- **Alle børnene er her.**
  All of the children are here.

65. **op** *prep* up
- **Løft mig op.**
  Lift me up.

66. **lade** *v* to let, allow
- **Lad mig vide, hvis du kan komme.**
  Let me know if you can come.

67. **hvorfor** *adv* why
- **Hvorfor kommer du for sent?**
  Why are you late?

68. **tro** *v* to believe
- **Jeg tror det er meget koldt.**
  I think that it is very cold.

69. **sig** *pro* himself, herself, etc. (third-person reflexive pronoun)
   - **Hun satte sig ned.**
     She sat (herself) down.

70. **tak** *int* thank you
   - **Tak for alt.**
     Thanks for everything.

71. **hvordan** *adv* how
   - **Hvordan har du det?**
     How are you?

72. **komme** *v* to come
   - **Undskyld. Jeg kan ikke komme i morgen.**
     Sorry. I can't come tomorrow.

73. **få** *v* to get, have
   - **Hun får alt, hvad hun ønsker.**
     She gets everything she wants.

74. **få** *adj* few
   - **Kun nogle få skal til paladset.**
     Only a few are going to the palace.

75. **kunne** *v* to be able, could, would, might
   - **Du skal kunne tale dansk for at få jobbet.**
     You must be able to speak Danish in order to get the job.

76. **meget** *adv* very, much
   - **Island er meget koldt.**
     Iceland is very cold.

77. **eller** *conj* or
   - **Kan du lide gul eller blå?**
     Do you like yellow or blue?

78. **hende** *pro* her (objective pronoun)
   - **Han elsker hende stadig.**
     He still loves her.

79. **ingen** *pro* no, no one, nobody
    - **Ingen af dem kom.**
    None of them came.

80. **tilbage** *adv* back, backwards
    - **Jeg ønsker ikke at gå tilbage.**
    I don't want to go back.

81. **hvem** *pro* who
    - **Hvem er den kvinde?**
    Who is that woman?

82. **gå** *v* to go
    - **Vi skal gå. Det er sent.**
    We should go. It is late.

83. **blive** *v* to become, be
    - **Han bliver vred.**
    He gets (becomes) angry.

84. **havde** *v* had (past tense of **have**)
    - **Vi havde et stort hus.**
    We had a large house.

85. **efter** *prep* after
    - **Hvad gør vi efter?**
    What are we doing after?

86. **nok** *adv* enough
    - **Er det nok?**
    Is that enough?

87. **man** *pro* one, you, people
    - **Kan man blive syg af vand?**
    Can you get sick from water?

88. **da** *conj* when, as, because
    - **Da jeg kom, gik hun.**
    As I arrived, she left.

89. **alt** *pro* everything
   - **Alt er dyrt her.**
   Everything is expensive here.

90. **sagde** *v* said (past tense of **sige**)
   - **Min far sagde nej.**
   My father said no.

91. **når** *conj* when
   - **Hun går i seng, når hun er søvnig.**
   She goes to bed when she is sleepy.

92. **ind** *adv* inside, in, into
   - **Kravl ind i kælderen.**
   Crawl into the basement.

93. **vores** *pro* our
   - **Vores børn er høje.**
   Our children are tall.

94. **over** *prep* above
   - **Hvad er over dit hoved?**
   What is above your head?

95. **aldrig** *adv* never
   - **Jeg vil aldrig tage derhen.**
   I will never go there.

96. **nogen** *pro* some, any, somebody, anybody
   - **Har vi nogen bananer?**
   Do we have any bananas?

97. **måske** *adv* perhaps, maybe
   - **Måske ikke i dag.**
   Maybe not today.

98. **hans** *pro* his
   - **Det er hans kæreste.**
   That is his girlfriend.

99. **skulle** *v* should, must, have to
- **Kampen vi skulle vinde.**
  We should win the battle.

100. **mand** *nc* man
- **Min far er en stor mand.**
  My father is a large man.

101. **selv** *adv* even
- **Selv en præst kan begå synder.**
  Even a priest can commit sins.

102. **selv** *pro* self (himself, herself etc.)
- **Bare vær dig selv.**
  Just be yourself.

103. **to** *num* two
- **Jeg har to brødre.**
  I have two brothers.

104. **mere** *adj* more
- **Jeg ønsker mere vand.**
  I want more water.

105. **jo** *adv* after all, obviously
- **Vi har jo ingen penge!**
  But we don't have any money!

106. **jo** *int* yes (used when answering a negative question)
- **A: Er du ikke svensk? B: Jo, jeg er svensk.**
  A: Aren't you Swedish? B: Yes, I am Swedish.

107. **jer** *pro* you (plural objective pronoun)
- **Jeg vil give det til jer.**
  I will give it to you (plural).

108. **sige** *v* to say, tell
- **Min mor siger "ja".**
  My mom says "yes".

109. **også** *adv* too, as well, also
- **Kommer hun også?**
  Is she also coming?

110. **lidt** *adj* a little, a bit
- **Jeg kan tale lidt dansk.**
  I can speak a little Danish.

111. **kun** *adv* only
- **Jeg kan kun læse lidt dansk.**
  I can only read a little Danish.

112. **deres** *pro* their
- **Deres chef er ond.**
  Their boss is mean.

113. **far** *nc* father, dad
- **Min far er dansk.**
  My father is Danish.

114. **blev** *v* was, became (past tense of **blive**)
- **Vi blev meget syge.**
  We got (became) very sick.

115. **hej** *int* hi, hello
- **Hej, Velkommen.**
  Hello, Welcome.

116. **sådan** *adj* such, like this, like that
- **Det er sådan, diktatorer begynder.**
  This is how dictators begin.

117. **dette** *pro* this
- **Denne film er meget lang.**
  This movie is very long.

118. **igen** *adv* again
- **Sig det igen.**
  Say it again.

119. **sammen** *adv* together
   - **Vi går overalt sammen.**
   We go everywhere together.

120. **denne** *pro* this, this one
   - **Denne sang er til dig.**
   This song is for you.

121. **hel** *adj* whole, full, entire
   - **Han spiste hele pizzaen.**
   He ate the whole pizza.

122. **tage** *v* to take, get, pick up, hold
   - **Tag en anden sandwich.**
   Take another sandwich.

123. **ned** *prep* down
   - **Sæt dig ned nu.**
   Sit down now.

124. **dag** *nc* day
   - **Det er en smuk dag.**
   It is a beautiful day.

125. **undskyld** *int* sorry, excuse me
   - **Undskyld, jeg forstår ikke.**
   Excuse me, I don't understand.

126. **mor** *nc* mother
   - **Min mor er norsk.**
   My mother is Norwegian.

127. **væk** *adv* gone, away
   - **Gå væk!**
   Go away!

128. **end** *conj* than
   - **Hun er klogere end mig.**
   She is smarter than me.

129. **været** *v* been (past participle of **være**)
- **Jeg kunne have været berømt.**
  I could have been famous.

130. **tid** *nc* time
- **Har du nogen tid?**
  Do you have any time?

131. **fordi** *conj* because
- **Vi gik tidligt, fordi vi var færdige.**
  We left early because we had finished.

132. **helt** *adv* completely, quite, totally
- **Jeg har helt glemt.**
  I completely forgot.

133. **sted** *nn* place, spot
- **Det er et dejligt sted.**
  This is a nice place.

134. **før** *prep* before
- **Hvad laver du før festen?**
  What are you doing before the party?

135. **gjorde** *v* did (past tense of **gøre**)
- **Hvad gjorde du?**
  What did you do?

136. **gang** *nc* time (occurrence)
- **Det er første gang.**
  This is the first time.

137. **år** *nn* year
- **Hvilket år blev du født?**
  What year were you born?

138. **lave** *v* to make, create, cook, prepare, do
- **Hvad laver du?**
  What are you doing?

139. **mange** *adj* many, a lot
   - **Hvor mange studerende er i din klasse?**
   How many students are in your class?

140. **nogle** *pro* some, some people (plural of **nogen**)
   - **Nogle ved ikke, hvordan man lever.**
   Some don't know how to live.

141. **fik** *v* got, had (past tense of **få**)
   - **Hun fik hjælp.**
   She got help.

142. **mene** *v* to mean
   - **Hvad mener du?**
   What do you mean?

143. **ting** *nc* thing, things
   - **Der har været så mange andre ting.**
   There have been so many other things.

144. **lille** *adj* small, little
   - **Denne kat er meget lille.**
   That cat is very little.

145. **siden** *adv* since
   - **Jeg har været i Danmark siden sidste år.**
   I have been in Denmark since last year.

146. **altid** *adv* always
   - **Middag er altid den samme.**
   Dinner is always the same.

147. **brug** *nc* use (**har brug for** - to need)
   - **Mit barn har brug for nye sko.**
   My child needs new shoes.

148. **folk** *nn* people
   - **Det danske folk er venlige.**
   The Danish people are friendly.

149. **virkelig** *adj* real, actual, really
- **Det er virkelig smukt i dag.**
  It is really beautiful today.

150. **vente** *v* to wait
- **At vente på sneen er en fryd og en forbandelse.**
  To wait for the snow is a delight and a curse.

151. **finde** *v* to find
- **Jeg kan ikke finde mine nøgler.**
  I can't find my keys.

152. **anden** *pro* other, another, else
- **Har du andre spørgsmål?**
  Do you have any other questions?

153. **anden** *num* second
- **Hvem er den anden højeste i klassen?**
  Who is the second tallest in the class?

154. **stadig** *adj* constant, steady
- **Er du stadig på arbejde?**
  Are you still at work?

155. **hjem** *nn* home
- **Jeg vil gerne hjem.**
  I want to go home.

156. **gud** *nc* god, (also used as a mild swear word)
- **Tror du på Gud?**
  Do you believe in God?

157. **liv** *nn* life
- **Jeg har et godt liv.**
  I have a good life.

158. **vej** *nc* road, way
- **Kender du vejen?**
  Do you know the way?

159. **kende** *v* to know (be familiar with)
- **Jeg kender denne by rigtig godt.**
  I know this city very well.

160. **andre** *pro* others
- **Hvor er de andre?**
  Where are the others?

161. **klar** *adj* ready
- **Er du klar?**
  Are you ready yet?

162. **tale** *nc* speech, talk
- **I talen, taler han om krig og kærlighed.**
  In the speech he talks about war and love.

163. **tale** *v* to speak, talk
- **Hun kan tale meget godt dansk.**
  She can speak very good Danish.

164. **mod** *prep* towards, against
- **Huset vender mod øst.**
  The house faces east.

165. **uden** *prep* without
- **Du kan gå uden mig.**
  You can go without me.

166. **elske** *v* to love
- **Jeg elsker mine børn.**
  I love my children.

167. **set** *v* seen (past participle of **se**)
- **Har du set min taske?**
  Have you seen my bag?

168. **tre** *num* three
- **Vi har tre hunde.**
  We have three dogs.

169. **høre** *v* to hear, listen
- **Kan du høre mig?**
  Can you hear me?

170. **ret** *adj* straight, right, proper
- **Er det en ret linje?**
  Is it a straight line?

171. **gerne** *adv* with pleasure, gladly
- **Jeg vil gerne have morgenmad.**
  I want to have breakfast.

172. **hr** *abb* Mr. (abbr. of **herr**)
- **Hr. Right tog fejl.**
  Mr. Right was wrong.

173. **give** *v* to give
- **Giv mig et sekund.**
  Give me a second.

174. **sidste** *adj* last
- **Det her er den sidste gang.**
  This is the last time.

175. **tog** *v* took (past tense of **tage**)
- **Han tog brødet.**
  He took the bread.

176. **tog** *nn* train
- **Hvad tid ankommer toget?**
  What time does the train arrive?

177. **fanden** *nc* Devil, Satan, damn
- **Å fanden. Jeg glemte noget.**
  Oh damn it. I forgot something.

178. **intet** *pro* nothing
- **Jeg så intet.**
  I saw nothing.

179. **død** *adj* dead
   - **Manden er død.**
     The man is dead.

180. **død** *nc* death
   - **Døden på fire hjul.**
     Death on four wheels.

181. **fint** *adv* alright
   - **Det er fint vejr.**
     The weather is fine.

182. **vel** *int* isn't it? (used as a tag question)
   - **Hun er ikke sur på mig, vel?**
     She isn't mad at me, is she?

183. **nå** *v* to reach, manage
   - **Jeg kan ikke nå den øverste hylde.**
     I can't reach the top shelf.

184. **jeres** *pro* your (plural)
   - **Hvor er jeres hus?**
     Where is your house?

185. **lide** *v* to suffer (**kunne lide** - to like)
   - **Jeg kan lide skiløb.**
     I like skiing.

186. **troede** *v* believed (past tense of **tro**)
   - **Jeg troede, det var mandag.**
     I thought that it was Monday.

187. **hendes** *pro* her (possessive)
   - **Hendes mand er dansk.**
     Her husband is Danish.

188. **hen** *adv* to (movement towards)
   - **Gå hen til din far.**
     Go to your father.

189. **blevet** *v* became, been, was (past participle of **blive**)
  * **Bogen er ikke blevet skrevet endnu.**
    The book hasn't been written yet.

190. **vide** *v* to know
  * **Jeg vil gerne vide mere om dig.**
    I want to know more about you.

191. **gjort** *v* done (past participle of **gøre**)
  * **Han har gjort det.**
    He has done it.

192. **ske** *v* to happen, occur, take place
  * **Hvad sker der her?**
    What is happening here?

193. **bedre** *adj* better
  * **Det er et meget bedre hus.**
    It is a much better house.

194. **ven** *nc* friend
  * **Hans er min bedste ven.**
    Hans is my best friend.

195. **første** *adj* first
  * **Er det dit første besøg?**
    Is this your first visit?

196. **hjælpe** *v* to help
  * **Kan du hjælpe mig?**
    Can you help me?

197. **aften** *nc* evening
  * **Jeg er træt om aftenen.**
    I am tired in the evening.

198. **samme** *adj* same, equal
  * **På samme tid**
    At the same time

199. **hjælp** *nc* help
- **Tak for din hjælp.**
  Thanks for your help.

200. **gik** *v* went, walked (past tense of **gå**)
- **Hun gik ind i værelset.**
  She walked into the room.

201. **vidste** *v* knew (past tense of **vide**)
- **Dét vidste jeg ikke.**
  I didn't know that.

202. **forstå** *v* to understand
- **Dansk er svært at forstå.**
  Danish is difficult to understand.

203. **arbejde** *v* to work
- **Hvor arbejder han?**
  Where does he work?

204. **under** *prep* under, below
- **Det er under bordet.**
  It is under the table.

205. **navn** *nn* name
- **Hvad er hendes navn?**
  What is her name?

206. **sin** *pro* his, her, its (own)
- **Han læser sin bog.**
  He reads his (own) book.

207. **eneste** *adj* only
- **Jeg er den eneste hjemme.**
  I am the only one home.

208. **penge** *npl* money
- **Hun har en masse penge.**
  She has a lot of money.

209. **morgen** *nc* morning
- **Jeg vågner tidligt om morgenen.**
  I wake up early in the morning.

210. **endnu** *adv* yet
- **Har du været i Frankrig endnu?**
  Have you been to France yet?

211. **burde** *v* should, ought to
- **Du burde få fikset det.**
  You should get it fixed.

212. **bedst** *adj* best
- **Hun er min bedste ven.**
  She is my best friend.

213. **bruge** *v* to use
- **Jeg er nødt til bruge computeren.**
  I need to use the computer.

214. **holde** *v* to hold, keep
- **Hvad holder du i hånden?**
  What are you holding in your hand?

215. **synes** *v* to think, seem, appear
- **Hvad synes du om mig?**
  What do you think about me?

216. **sikker** *adj* safe, sure
- **Danmark er et sikkert land.**
  Denmark is a safe country.

217. **fortælle** *v* to tell, report
- **Fortæl mig sandheden.**
  Tell me the truth.

218. **stå** *v* to stand
- **Stå op!**
  Stand up!

219. **stoppe** *v* to stop
- **At stoppe med at beklage mig virker umuligt.**
  To stop complaining seems impossible.

220. **sikkert** *adv* probably
- **De kender sikkert ikke svaret.**
  They probably don't know the answer.

221. **nødt** *adj* need (**er nødt** - to need, have to)
- **Jeg er nødt til at studere på denne eftermiddag.**
  I have to study this afternoon.

222. **længe** *adv* long
- **Hvor længe må jeg parkere her?**
  How long may I park here?

223. **verden** *nc* world
- **Hvor mange børn er der i verden?**
  How many children are there in the world?

224. **engang** *adv* once, one day, sometime
- **Der var engang ...**
  Once upon a time ...

225. **stor** *adj* large, great
- **Rusland er et meget stort land.**
  Russia is a very large country.

226. **døde** *v* died (past tense of **dø**)
- **Mange mennesker døde i ulykken.**
  Many people died in the accident.

227. **hver** *pro* every, each, everyone
- **Jeg drikker kaffe hver morgen.**
  I drink coffee every morning.

228. **måde** *nc* method, way
- **Gør det på den her måde.**
  Do it this way.

229. **fyr** *nc* guy, chap, bloke
- **Hvem er den fyr?**
  Who is that guy?

230. **ude** *adv* out, outside
- **Hun er ude af landet.**
  She is out of the country.

231. **hedde** *v* to be called (have a specific name)
- **Hvad hedder du?**
  What is your name?

232. **par** *nn* pair, couple
- **De er et dejligt par.**
  They are a lovely couple.

233. **fandt** *v* found (past tense of **finde**)
- **De fandt deres bil.**
  They found their car.

234. **selvfølgelig** *adv* of course, naturally
- **Selvfølgelig kan jeg tale dansk.**
  Of course I can speak Danish.

235. **fået** *v* gotten (past participle of **få**)
- **Hun er hjemme, fordi hun har fået influenza.**
  She is at home because she has caught the flu.

236. **bange** *adj* afraid, scared
- **Hvad er du bange for?**
  What are you afraid of?

237. **først** *adv* at first, only
- **Dette er mit første job.**
  This is my first job.

238. **snart** *adv* soon
- **Filmen starter snart.**
  The movie is going to start soon.

239. **næste** *adj* next, the following
  * **I næste uge er det min ferie.**
    Next week is my vacation.

240. **disse** *pro* these, these ones
  * **Disse småkager er lækre.**
    These cookies are delicious.

241. **øjeblik** *nn* moment
  * **Vent et øjeblik.**
    Wait a moment.

242. **faktisk** *adj* actual, real, as a matter of fact
  * **På Island er det faktisk ikke særlig koldt.**
    Iceland is not actually very cold.

243. **mænd** *nc* men (plural of **mand**)
  * **Der er fem mænd på kontoret.**
    There are five men in the office.

244. **ihjel** *adv* to death (e.g. bored to death)
  * **Han blev slået ihjel.**
    He was beaten to death.

245. **behøve** *v* to need, have to
  * **Du behøver ikke at komme.**
    You don't have to come.

246. **betyde** *v* to mean
  * **Hvad betyder dette ord?**
    What does this work mean?

247. **pige** *nc* girl
  * **Der er ti piger i klassen.**
    There are ten girls in the class.

248. **hos** *prep* at, by, with
  * **Jeg bor hos mine forældre.**
    I live with my parents.

249. **ellers** *adv* otherwise
- **Besøg ambasaden først ellers kommer du ingen vegne.**
  Visit the embassy first otherwise you'll get nowhere.

250. **flere** *adj* more, other
- **Jeg har flere brødre end søstre.**
  I have more brothers than sisters.

251. **lort** *nc* (vulgar) crap, shit
- **Det her hotel er noget lort!**
  This hotel is crap!

252. **gamle** *adj* old (plural of **gammel**)
- **Bøgerne er gamle.**
  The books are old.

253. **kede** *v* to be bored
- **Jeg keder mig.**
  I'm bored.

254. **søn** *nc* son
- **Min søn bor i Tyskland.**
  My son lives in Germany.

255. **hallo** *int* hello (answering a phone)
- **Hallo, det er Jean.**
  Hello, it's Jean speaking.

256. **prøve** *v* to try, test
- **Kan jeg prøve på denne kjole?**
  Can I try on this dress?

257. **ligesom** *adv* sort of, kind of
- **Kan man træne en kat ligesom en hund?**
  Can you train a cat like a dog?

258. **stille** *adj* still, quiet, calm
- **Det er en stille nat.**
  It is a quiet night.

259. **menneske** *nn* person, human
- **Til hvor mange mennesker?**
  For how many people?

260. **dø** *v* to die
- **Det vil være trist, hvis deres hund dør.**
  It will be sad if their dog dies.

261. **ny** *adj* new
- **Mine nye sko er komfortable.**
  My new shoes are comfortable.

262. **børn** *nn* children (plural of **barn**)
- **Vi har tre børn.**
  We have three children.

263. **vist** *adv* shown (past participle of **vise**)
- **Så du filmen der blev vist i fjernsynet i aftes?**
  Did you see the film that was shown on TV last night?

264. **minutter** *nn* minutes
- **En time har tres minutter.**
  An hour has sixty minutes.

265. **slå** *v* to hit, beat
- **Hun slår ham.**
  She is hitting him.

266. **gav** *v* gave (past tense of **give**)
- **Hun gav mig et kort.**
  She gave me a card.

267. **fem** *num* five
- **Min familie har fem børn.**
  My family has five children.

268. **huske** *v* to remember
- **Jeg husker din fødselsdag.**
  I remember your birthday.

269. **galt** *adv* wrong
- **Hvad er der galt med dig?**
  What is wrong with you?

270. **derfor** *adv* therefore
- **Jeg tænker derfor er jeg.**
  I think therefore I am.

271. **orden** *nc* neatness, order
- **Min bil er ikke i orden.**
  My car is not clean (in order).

272. **rigtig** *adj* right, correct, true
- **Rigtigt eller forkert?**
  True or false?

273. **gange** *nc* times (occurrences)
- **Jeg har været der mange gange.**
  I have been there many times.

274. **pas** *nn* passport
- **Er et pas en adgang til hele verden?**
  Is a passport is an access to the whole world?

275. **helvede** *nn* hell
- **Jeg føler, at jeg lever i helvede.**
  I feel like I'm living in hell.

276. **kone** *nc* wife
- **Jeg elsker min kone.**
  I love my wife.

277. **fundet** *adv* found (past participle of **finde**)
- **Har du fundet det endnu?**
  Have you found it yet?

278. **alene** *adj* alone
- **Jeg hader at være alene.**
  I hate to be alone.

279. **farvel** *int* goodbye
- **Farvel alle!**
  Goodbye everyone!

280. **møde** *nn* meeting
- **Jeg er for sent på den til mit møde.**
  I am late for my meeting.

281. **møde** *v* to meet
- **Det er en ære at møde dig.**
  It's an honour to meet you.

282. **allerede** *adv* already
- **Er han allerede taget afsted?**
  Has he already left?

283. **hurtigt** *adv* quickly, fast
- **Hun kan løbe meget hurtigt.**
  She can run very fast.

284. **én** *num* one
- **Én kvinde er ladt tilbage.**
  One woman is left behind.

285. **herfra** *adv* from here
- **Det tager en time at gå herfra.**
  It takes one hour to walk from here.

286. **ønske** *v* to wish
- **Jeg ønsker at rejse rundt i verden.**
  I want to travel around the world.

287. **grund** *nc* reason, cause
- **Der er ingen grund til at risikere det.**
  There is no reason to risk it.

288. **slags** *nc* kind, sort, type
- **Der findes to slags mennesker her i verden.**
  There are two types of people in the world.

289. **rolig** *adj* calm, quiet
- **Dette er et roligt kvarter.**
  This is a quiet neighborhood.

290. **hvilken** *pro* what, which, who, whom
- **Hvilken bil er din?**
  Which car is yours?

291. **altså** *part* well then, and so, that is
- **Hun kommer altså ikke?**
  So, she's not coming?

292. **bil** *nn* car, automobile
- **Jeg har brug for en ny bil.**
  I need a new car.

293. **skylder** *v* to owe (have debt)
- **Min onkel skylder en masse penge.**
  My uncle owes a lot of money.

294. **familie** *nc* family
- **Jeg har en stor familie.**
  I have a large family.

295. **sagt** *v* said (past participle of **sige**)
- **Jeg tror, jeg har sagt et eller andet galt.**
  I think I have said something wrong.

296. **kvinde** *nc* woman
- **Den kvinde er meget smuk.**
  That woman is very beautiful.

297. **fire** *num* four
- **Det er klokken fire.**
  It is four o'clock.

298. **klare** *v* to manage, handle, cope
- **Kan hun ikke klare det?**
  Can she not handle it?

299. **dræbe** *v* to kill
- **Han dræbte tre mennesker.**
  He killed three people.

300. **dreng** *nc* boy
- **Jeg har to drenge.**
  I have two boys.

301. **hvornår** *adv* when
- **Hvornår ankommer toget?**
  When does the train arrive?

302. **rundt** *adv* around
- **Han kører rundt i nabolaget.**
  He drives around the neighbourhood.

303. **imod** *præp* against, opposed to
- **Hvem har du spillet imod?**
  Who did you play against?

304. **dør** *nc* door
- **Åben døren.**
  Open the door.

305. **frem** *adv* forward, toward
- **For det første ser jeg frem til at komme.**
  For the first time I look forward to coming.

306. **senere** *adv* later
- **Vi ses senere.**
  See you later.

307. **langt** *adv* far
- **Han bor langt væk.**
  He lives far away.

308. **del** *nc* part, portion, section
- **Det er i to dele.**
  It is in two parts.

309. **begge** *pro* both
- **Begge biler er gule.**
  Both cars are yellow.

310. **håbe** *v* to hope
- **Jeg håber at du har det godt.**
  I hope that you are doing well.

311. **fejl** *nc* mistake, error
- **Det er selvfølgelig en fejl.**
  It's obviously a mistake.

312. **inden** *prep* before
- **Pak grundigt inden du rejser.**
  Pack carefully before you travel.

313. **nogensinde** *adv* ever, at some time
- **Jeg tror ikke, hun nogensinde smiler.**
  I don't think she ever smiles.

314. **glad** *adj* happy, glad
- **De er meget glade i dag.**
  They are very happy today.

315. **køre** *v* to drive
- **Kan han køre en lastbil?**
  Can he drive a truck?

316. **heller** *adv* rather
- **Jeg vil hellere blive blind end at miste dig.**
  I'd rather go blind than to lose you.

317. **sand** *adj* true
- **Er hvad han sagde sandt?**
  Is what he said true?

318. **hinanden** *pro* each other
- **De elsker hinanden.**
  They love each other.

319. **næsten** *adv* nearly, almost
   - **Det er næsten midnat.**
     It is almost midnight.

320. **inde** *adv* inside
   - **Hvilket bogstav er inde i cirklen?**
     Which letter is inside the circle?

321. **virke** *v* to seem, appear, function properly
   - **Det spil virker meget kompliceret.**
     That game seems very complicated.

322. **leder** *nc* leader, manager
   - **I mit erhverv som leder af en skole.**
     In my profession as head of a school.

323. **hus** *nn* house
   - **Vi elsker vores hus.**
     We love our house.

324. **kæft** *nc* (vulgar) mouth (**holde kæft** - shut up)
   - **Jeg kan simpelthen ikke holde min kæft.**
     I cannot simply keep my mouth shut.

325. **ord** *nn* word
   - **Hvor mange ord kender du?**
     How many words do you know?

326. **ingenting** *pro* nothing
   - **De har ingenting at gøre i Jylland.**
     They have nothing to do in Jutland.

327. **politi** *nn* police
   - **Ring til politiet!**
     Call the police!

328. **gået** *v* gone (past participle of **gå**)
   - **Kvinden er gået.**
     The woman has gone.

329. **spørgsmål** *nn* question
- **Du kan stille mig et spørgsmål.**
  You can ask me a question.

330. **lang** *adj* long (distance)
- **Gaden er meget lang.**
  The street is very long.

331. **time** *nc* hour
- **Toget vil ankomme inden for en time.**
  The train will arrive in one hour.

332. **snakke** *v* to talk, speak
- **Kan du snakke engelsk?**
  Can you speak English?

333. **lyd** *nc* sound
- **Det lyder godt.**
  It sounds great.

334. **bag** *prep, adv* behind
- **Vi er bag dig.**
  We are behind you.

335. **bror** *nc* brother
- **Hun har en bror.**
  She has a brother.

336. **kaptajn** *nc* captain
- **Han er en kaptajn.**
  He is a captain.

337. **problem** *nn* problem
- **Dette er et stort problem.**
  This is a big problem.

338. **indtil** *conj* until
- **Jeg bliver indtil klokken seks.**
  I am staying until six o'clock.

339. **dog** *conj* though
- **Det er dog mærkeligt, at hendes børn ikke er her.**
  However, it is strange that her kids are not here.

340. **tænkte** *v* thought (past tense of **tænke**)
- **Jeg tænkte ikke over dét.**
  I didn't think about that.

341. **videre** *adv* further, farther
- **Du må gå videre, hvis du vil være lykkelig.**
  You have to go further if you want to be happy.

342. **sent** *adv* late
- **De er altid sent på den.**
  They are always late.

343. **ben** *nn* leg, bone
- **Han brækkede benet.**
  He broke his leg.

344. **sød** *adj* sweet, pretty, cute
- **Hvalpen er sød.**
  The puppy is cute.

345. **løbe** *v* to run
- **Jeg ønsker at løbe en maraton.**
  I want to run a marathon.

346. **egen** *adj* own
- **Brug dine egne ord.**
  Use your own words.

347. **ond** *adj* bad, evil
- **Hvem er egentlig ond?**
  Who is really evil?

348. **barn** *nn* child
- **De vil have et barn.**
  They want a child.

349. **velkommen** *int* welcome
- **Velkommen til Danmark.**
  Welcome to Denmark.

350. **vise** *v* to show
- **Kan du vise mig dit billede?**
  Can you show me your picture.

351. **mens** *conj* while
- **Mens jeg løb, regnede det.**
  While I ran, it rained.

352. **omkring** *adj* about, around
- **Det er omkring huset.**
  It is around the house.

353. **igennem** *adv* through
- **At komme igennem menneskemængden var vanskeligt.**
  Getting through the crowd was difficult.

354. **fortalte** *v* told (past tense of **fortælle**)
- **Han fortalte mig at jeg aldrig ville få en uddannelse.**
  He told me that I would never get an education.

355. **slap** *adj* let go, release (past tense of **slippe**)
- **Men med hendes hjælp slap han fri.**
  But with her help, he was set free.

356. **forbi** *adv* finished, past
- **Mødet er forbi.**
  The meeting is over.

357. **gennem** *prep* through
- **Følg stien gennem parken.**
  Follow the path through the park.

358. **kalde** *v* to call, refer to
- **De kalder det "sms'e".**
  They call it "texting".

359. **job** *nn* job, work
- **Det er svært at finde et godt job.**
  It is hard to find a good job.

360. **tænke** *v* to think
- **At tænke på isolationen er svært.**
  To think about the isolation is tough.

361. **ti** *num* ten
- **Jeg har ti fingre.**
  I have ten fingers.

362. **fri** *adj* free
- **Vi har brug for en fri presse.**
  We need a free press.

363. **gammel** *adj* old
- **Historien er gammel.**
  The story is old.

364. **ringe** *v* to call (on the telephone)
- **Ring til mig senere.**
  Call me later.

365. **sjov** *adj* fun
- **Fodbold er en sjov sport.**
  Football is a fun sport.

366. **færdig** *adj* finished, completed
- **Filmen er færdig.**
  The movie is finished.

367. **fast** *adj* firm, solid, fixed
- **Lad os derfor slå helt fast, at situationen stadig er alvorlig.**
  Let us make it very clear, the situation continues to be serious.

368. **våben** *nn* weapon
- **En pistol er et våben.**
  A pistol is a weapon.

369. **chance** *nc* chance
- **Giv mig en endnu chance.**
  Give me another chance.

370. **kører** *nc* driver
- **"Vi er her" sagde køreren.**
  "We are here" said the driver.

371. **ligne** *v* to resemble, look like, be like
- **Den kvinde ligner min søster.**
  That woman looks like my sister.

372. **bad** *v* asked, requested (past tense of **bede**)
- **De bad mig om at være stille.**
  They asked me to be quiet.

373. **bad** *nn* bath, bathroom
- **De har brug for at komme i bad.**
  They need to get in the bath.

374. **al** *pro* all, any
- **Al medicinen er væk.**
  All the medicine is gone.

375. **sidde** *v* to sit
- **Alle de studerende sidder.**
  The students are all sitting.

376. **ligge** *v* to lie (horizontal position), to be (occupy a place)
- **Jeg er træt. Jeg ligger ned.**
  I am tired. I am lying down.

377. **hånd** *nc* hand
- **Der er fem fingre på min hånd.**
  There are five fingers on my hand.

378. **mad** *nc* food
- **Har du noget mad i køleskabet?**
  Do we have any food in the refrigerator?

379. **hjemme** *adv* home, at home
- **Er du alene hjemme?**
  Are you home alone?

380. **hade** *v* to hate
- **Hun hader slanger.**
  She hates snakes.

381. **mest** *adj* most
- **De har sovet det meste af dagen.**
  They slept most of the day.

382. **seks** *num* six
- **Min søster har seks katte.**
  My sister has six cats.

383. **sgu** *adv* (vulgar intensifier) damn
- **Jeg tror sgu, vi har fat i noget.**
  I think damn, we got something.

384. **historie** *nc* history, story
- **Det er en lang historie.**
  It's a long story.

385. **nummer** *nn* number
- **Han bærer nummer fem.**
  He wears number five.

386. **flot** *adj* fine, great
- **Det er flot!**
  That's great!

387. **plads** *nc* place, room, position
- **Vores værelse er lille. Der er ikke meget plads.**
  Our room is small. There isn't much room.

388. **hoved** *nn* head
- **Han har et stort hoved.**
  He has a big head.

389. **datter** *nc* daughter
- **Det er min ældste datter.**
  That is my eldest daughter.

390. **svær** *adj* difficult, hard
- **Kinesisk er et svært sprog.**
  Chinese is a difficult language.

391. **føle** *v* to feel, touch
- **Jeg føler mig lidt trist.**
  I'm feeling a little sad.

392. **beklage** *v* to regret, be sorry
- **Jeg beklager ulejligheden.**
  I apologize for the inconvenience.

393. **fantastisk** *adj* incredible, amazing, fantastic
- **Partiet var fantastisk.**
  The party was fantastic.

394. **bo** *v* to live, reside
- **Han bor i København.**
  He lives in Copenhagen.

395. **slet** *part* at all
- **Jeg er slet ikke sikker.**
  I am not at all sure.

396. **nat** *nc* night
- **Det er en mørk nat.**
  It is a dark night.

397. **helst** *adv* anything, anyone, whatever
- **Der er ingen grund til at tale med nogen som helst.**
  There is no need to talk to anyone.

398. **leve** *v* to live, be alive
- **Lever din fisk stadig?**
  Is your fish still alive?

399. **mellem** *prep* between, among
- **Bare mellem dig og mig.**
  Just between you and me.

400. **glemme** *v* to forget
- **Glem ikke dit jubilæum.**
  Don't forget your anniversary.

401. **redde** *v* to save
- **Vi kan ikke redde hele verden.**
  We cannot save the whole world.

402. **tæt** *adj* close
- **Jeg er meget tæt på min søster.**
  I am very close to my sister.

403. **blod** *nn* blood
- **Jeg fik blod på min skjorte.**
  I got blood on my shirt.

404. **jorden** *nc* the Earth
- **Jorden er den tredje planet fra Solen.**
  The Earth is the third planet from the Sun.

405. **spise** *v* to eat
- **Hvad har du lyst til at spise?**
  What do you want to eat?

406. **herre** *nc* sir, mister
- **Han er en ældre herre.**
  He is an older gentleman.

407. **uge** *nc* week
- **Der er 52 uger på et år.**
  There are 52 weeks in a year.

408. **vand** *nn* water
- **Et glas vand, tak.**
  A glass of water, thanks.

409. **tur** *nc* walk, trip, tour
- **Lad os gå en tur.**
  Let's go for a walk.

410. **kort** *adj* short, brief
- **Du kan læse den. Bogen er meget kort.**
  You can read it. The book is very short.

411. **sag** *nc* matter, business, case
- **Dette er en vanskelig sag at løse.**
  This is a difficult case to solve.

412. **passe** *v* to look after
- **Hun passer på sin lillebror.**
  She looks after her younger sister.

413. **øjne** *nn* eyes
- **Hun har brune øjne.**
  She has brown eyes.

414. **lære** *v* to teach, learn
- **Jeg lærer dansk.**
  I am learning Danish.

415. **spille** *v* to play
- **Børnene spiller fodbold i haven.**
  The children are playing football in the garden.

416. **gift** *adj* married
- **Er du gift?**
  Are you married?

417. **søster** *nc* sister
- **Jeg har en søster.**
  I have a sister.

418. **små** *adj* small, little (plural of **lille**)
- **Er dine børn stadig små?**
  Are your children still small?

419. **mindre** *adj* less
- **Vi er nødt til at bruge færre penge.**
  We need to spend less money.

420. **begynde** *v* to start, begin
- **Vær stille. Filmen begynder.**
  Be quiet. The movie is starting.

421. **forstået** *v* understood (past participle of **forstå**)
- **Er det forstået?**
  Is that understood?

422. **fuld** *adj* full
- **Skålen er fuld.**
  The bowl is full.

423. **hjerte** *nn* heart
- **Hun har et stort hjerte.**
  She has a big heart.

424. **holdt** *v* held, kept (past tense of **holde**)
- **Hun holdt min hånd.**
  She held my hand.

425. **måtte** *v* had to (**måtte** is present and past tense)
- **Jeg måtte forlade byen.**
  I had to leave the city.

426. **præcis** *adj* precise, exactly
- **Det er præcis det, jeg taler om.**
  That is exactly what I'm talking about.

427. **bør** *v* should, ought to (present tense of **burde**)
- **Du bør ikke gøre det.**
  You shouldn't do that.

428. **land** *nn* country (nation state)
- **Danmark er et lille land.**
  Denmark is a small country.

429. **by** *nc* city
- **London er en stor by.**
  London is a large city.

430. **øje** *nn* eye
- **Jeg har fået noget i øjet.**
  I have something in my eye.

431. **lov** *nc* law
- **Er dansk lov anderledes end svensk?**
  Is Danish law different than Swedish?

432. **skynde** *v* to hurry
- **Skynd dig! Du er sent på den.**
  Hurry up! You are late.

433. **slut** *adj* over, finished
- **Festen er slut.**
  The party is over.

434. **fred** *nc* peace
- **De ønsker fred.**
  They want peace.

435. **smuk** *adj* beautiful, handsome
- **De har et smukt hus.**
  They have a beautiful house.

436. **sandhed** *nc* truth
- **Han fortæller mig ikke sandheden.**
  He is not telling me the truth.

437. **klokken** *nc* o'clock
- **Jeg er nødt til være hjemme klokken fem.**
  I need to be home at five o'clock.

438. **spørge** *v* to ask, inquire
- **Jeg vil gerne spørge dig om noget.**
  I want to ask you something.

439. **fed** *adj* fat
- **Han bliver lidt fed.**
  He is getting a little fat.

440. **værsgo** *int* here you are
- **Drikke en øl. Værsgo.**
  Have a beer. Here you go.

441. **kære** *adj* dear
- **Tak min kære.**
  Thank you my dear.

442. **slog** *v* hit (past tense of **slå**)
- **Han slog ham i ansigtet.**
  He hit him in the face.

443. **held** *nn* luck, fortune
- **Held og lykke med testen.**
  Good luck on the test.

444. **kæreste** *nc* boyfriend or girlfriend
- **Har du en kæreste?**
  Do you have a boyfriend (girlfriend)?

445. **ung** *adj* young
- **Præsidenten er meget ung.**
  The president is very young.

446. **knægt** *nc* boy, lad
- **Det er historien om en lille knægt fra København.**
  This is the story of a little boy from Copenhagen.

447. **alligevel** *adv* nonetheless, anyway
- **Men han sagde, at det alligevel ikke var hende.**
  But he said it wasn't her anyway.

448. **nede** *adv* down
- **Der ligger en ny restaurant nede på hjørnet.**
  There is a new restaurant down on the corner.

449. **herrer** *nc* gentlemen
- **Mine damer og herrer!**
  Ladies and Gentlemen!

450. **besked** *nc* message
- **Har han lagt en besked?**
  Did he leave a message?

451. **slippe** *v* to drop, let something fall
- **Du kan trække og slippe.**
  You can drag and drop.

452. **roligt** *adv* calmly, quietly, easily
- **Tag det nu roligt!**
  Take it easy!

453. **valg** *nn* election, choice
- **Der er valg i Danmark.**
  There is an election in Denmark.

454. **tænkt** *v* thought (past participle of **tænke**)
- **Det har jeg ikke tænkt på endnu.**
  I haven't thought of that yet.

455. **findes** *v* to exist
- **Der findes intet smukkere end isbjerge!**
  There is nothing more beautiful than icebergs!

456. **oppe** *adv* up
- **Da jeg kom hjem, var både Kristina og børnene oppe.**
  When I got home, both Kristina and the children were up.

457. **seng** *nc* bed
- **Jeg ønsker at købe en ny seng.**
  I want to buy a new bed.

458. **kærlighed** *nc* love
- **Kærlighed er smukt.**
  Love is beautiful.

459. **måned** *nc* month
- **Der er tolv måneder på et år.**
  There are twelve months in a year.

460. **svin** *nn* pig
- **Landmanden har en masse svin.**
  The farmer has a lot of pigs.

461. **masse** *nc* a lot, lots
- **Der var en masse billeder.**
  There were a lot of pictures.

462. **sætte** *v* to put, place, set
- **Han vil have mig til at sætte mad på bordet.**
  He wants me to put food on the table.

463. **perfekt** *adj* perfect
- **Denne kage er perfekt.**
  This cake is perfect.

464. **tom** *adj* empty
- **Min kop er tom.**
  My cup is empty.

465. **foran** *prep* in front of
- **Hvad er foran denne bygning?**
  What is in front of that building?

466. **idé** *nc* idea
- **Det er en fantastisk idé.**
  That is a fantastic idea.

467. **fortalt** *v* told (past participle of **fortælle**)
- **Hvad har du fået fortalt?**
  What have you been told?

468. **muligt** *adj* possible
- **Alt er muligt.**
  Anything is possible.

469. **ansigt** *nn* face
- **Han har et ar i sit ansigt.**
  He has a scar on his face.

470. **forkert** *adj* wrong
- **Din chef er forkert på den igen.**
  Your boss is wrong again.

471. **rejse** *v* to travel
- **Vi elsker at rejse.**
  We love traveling.

472. **rejse** *nc* journey, trip
- **Det var skibets første rejse.**
  It was the ship's first journey.

473. **elskede** *nc* darling, beloved
- **Hallo! Hej min elskede!**
  Hello! Hi my love!

474. **røv** *nc* (vulgar) ass, arse
- **Hun sparker røv!**
  She kicks ass!

475. **lyst** *nc* inclination, desire, want
- **Jeg har kun lyst at være sammen med dig.**
  I only want to be with you.

476. **stykke** *nn* piece
- **Vil du have et stykke?**
  Do you want another piece?

477. **krig** *nc* war
- **Der er krig i Syrien.**
  There is a war in Syria.

478. **foregå** *v* to happen, going on
- **Hvad foregår der?**
  What is going on?

479. **vigtig** *adj* important
- **Uddannelse er vigtig.**
  Education is important.

480. **aftale** *nc* arrangement, agreement, deal
- **Jeg har en aftale med lægen.**
  I have an appointment with the doctor.

481. **aftale** *v* to arrange
- **Kan du aftale et møde?**
  Can you arrange a meeting?

482. **venstre** *adj* left (direction)
- **Drej til venstre.**
  Turn left.

483. **endelig** *adv* finally, eventually
- **Jeg endelig fundet mine briller.**
  I finally found my glasses.

484. **idiot** *nc* idiot
- **Jeg er ked af, hvis jeg har været en idiot.**
  I am sorry if I've been an idiot.

485. **goddag** *int* good day, hello
- **Goddag. Hvordan har du det?**
  Hello. How are you?

486. **svar** *nn* answer, response
- **Hun gav mig endelig et svar.**
  She finally gave me an answer.

487. **spil** *nn* game
- **Børnene spiller et spil.**
  The children are playing a game.

488. **ønske** *nn* wish
- **Har du et ønske?**
  Did you have a wish?

489. **plan** *nc* plan
- **Så hvad er planen?**
  So what is the plan?

490. **hård** *adj* hard, tough, harsh
- **Mit sæde er for hårdt.**
  My seat is too hard.

491. **kamp** *nc* fight, battle, match
- **Hvem vandt kampen?**
  Who won the match?

492. **sikkerhed** *nc* safety
- **Sikkerhed i dit nabolag er vigtig.**
  Safety in your neighbourhood is important.

493. **million** *num* million
- **Han er millioner af kroner værd.**
  He is worth millions of kroner.

494. **chef** *nc* boss, person in charge
- **Jeg har en irriterende chef.**
  I have an annoying boss.

495. **skyde** *v* to shoot
- **Han kan skyde med pistol.**
  He can shoot a gun.

496. **højre** *adj* right (direction)
- **Drej til højre ved hjørnet.**
  Turn right at the corner.

497. **lykke** *nc* happiness, luck
- **Held og lykke!**
  Good luck!

498. **mening** *nc* opinion, meaning
- **Efter min mening er det for stort.**
  In my opinion it is too big.

499. **værelse** *nn* room
- **Der er tre værelser i deres lejlighed.**
  There are three rooms in their apartment.

500. **godmorgen** *int* good morning
- **Godmorgen kære.**
  Good morning dear.

501. **derude** *adv* out there
- **Vi har været derude i dag.**
  We have been out there today.

502. **betale** *v* to pay (give money)
- **Han betaler for mig i dag.**
  He is paying for me today.

503. **trække** *v* to pull
- **Kan du trækker vognen?**
  Can you pull the wagon?

504. **klart** *adv* clearly
- **Han er helt klart ikke den rette person.**
  He is clearly not the right person.

505. **bede** *v* to ask, request, pray
- **Jeg har brug for at bede hende om en tjeneste.**
  I need to ask her for a favor.

506. **hænder** *nc* hands
- **Mine hænder er kolde.**
  My hands are cold.

507. **godnat** *int* good night
- **Godnat min elskede.**
  Goodnight my love.

508. **kæmpe** *v* to fight, struggle
- **Brødre kæmper altid.**
  Brothers always fight.

509. **blot** *adv* only, merely
- **Hvis jeg blot havde mere tid.**
  If I only had more time.

510. **fly** *nn* airplane
- **Piloten flyver flyet.**
  The pilot flies the airplane.

511. **ligeglad** *adj* indifferent, don't care
- **Jeg er ligeglad med, hvad det koster.**
  I don't care what it costs.

512. **film** *nc* movie, film
- **Det var en lang film.**
  That was a long movie.

513. **talte** *v* spoke, told (past tense of **tale**)
- **Talte du med ham?**
  Did you speak with him?

514. **hente** *v* to fetch
- **Jeg henter det.**
  I'll go and fetch it.

515. **syv** *num* seven
- **Der er syv dage på en uge.**
  There are seven days in a week.

516. **pistol** *nc* handgun, pistol
- **Tyven har en pistol.**
  The thief had a gun.

517. **værd** *adj* worth
- **Hvad er den bil værd?**
  What is that car worth?

518. **forældre** *nc* parents
- **Min bror bor hos vores forældre.**
  My brother lives with our parents.

519. **gut** *nc* boy, guy, bloke
- **Det er en god sport for unge gutter.**
  This is a good sport for young boys.

520. **rar** *adj* pleasant, kind, nice
- **Hans datter er meget rar.**
  His daughter is very nice.

521. **let** *adj* easy
- **Dette spil er meget let.**
  This game is very easy.

522. **vinde** *v* to win
- **Hvis jeg vinder i lotteriet.**
  If I win the lottery.

523. **ane** *nc* ancestor, forefather
- **Jeg er amerikansk, men jeg har danske aner.**
  I am American but I have Danish ancestors.

524. **tøj** *nn* clothes, clothing
- **Hun har dyrt tøj.**
  She has expensive clothes.

525. **værre** *adj* worse
- **Fra slemt til værre.**
  From bad to worse.

526. **talt** *v* spoken, told (past participle of **tale**)
- **Har du talt med ham endnu?**
  Have you spoken with him yet?

527. **fald** *nn* fall, decrease
- **Vi havde et fald i salget.**
  We had a fall in sales.

528. **dårligt** *adv* badly, poorly
- **Hun er en nybegynder. Hun taler dårligt.**
  She is a beginner. She speaks poorly.

529. **dum** *adj* stupid, foolish
- **De er dumme turister.**
  They are dumb tourists.

530. **sove** *v* to sleep
- **Rolige. Han sover.**
  Quiet. He is sleeping.

531. **hvid** *adj* white
- **Sne er hvid.**
  Snow is white.

532. **træt** *adj* tired
- **Jeg er så træt.**
  I am so tired.

533. **tidligere** *adj* former
- **Hvad siger den tidligere præsident?**
  What does the former president say?

534. **derinde** *adv* in there
- **Hvad sker der derinde?**
  What's happening in there?

535. **stod** *v* stood (past tense of **stå**)
- **Hunden stod stille i lang tid.**
  The dog stood still for a long time.

536. **straks** *adv* at once, immediately
- **Okay. Er straks tilbage.**
  Okay. Be right back.

537. **købe** *v* to buy
- **Jeg har brug for at købe frokost.**
  I need to buy lunch.

538. **skrive** *v* to write
- **Hun skriver et brev.**
  She writes a letter.

539. **følge** *v* to follow
- **Stop med at følge efter mig.**
  Stop following me.

540. **største** *adj* largest, biggest, greatest
- **Rusland er det største land i verden.**
  Russia is the largest country in the world.

541. **mindst** *adv* least, at least
- **Mindst femten mennesker blev såret.**
  At least fifteen people were injured.

542. **kendte** *v* knew (past tense of **kende**)
- **Jeg så slet ingen, jeg kendte.**
  I saw no one that I knew.

543. **person** *nc* person
- **Hun er den rette person til jobbet.**
  She is the right person for the job.

544. **mærke** *nn* mark, brand
- **Kan danske mærker fås i Amerika?**
  Are Danish brands available in America?

545. **gide** *v* to be bothered, to care
- **Jeg gider ikke at rense badeværelset.**
  I cannot be bothered to clean the bathroom.

546. **lys** *nn* light
- **Sluk lyset, tak.**
  Turn of the light, thanks.

547. **sekund** *nc* second
- **Et minut har tres sekunder.**
  A minute has sixty seconds.

548. **hund** *nc* dog
- **Min nabo har to hunde.**
  My neighbor has two dogs.

549. **desværre** *adv* regrettably, unfortunately
- **Desværre, min mobil er død.**
  Unfortunately my cell phone is dead.

550. **nød** *v* enjoyed (past tense of **nyde**)
- **Han var en dreng, der nød opmærksomheden.**
  He was a boy that enjoyed the attention.

551. **skudt** *v* shot (past participle of **skyde**)
- **Hjælp! Han er blevet skudt.**
  Help! He has been shot.

552. **utroligt** *adv* incredibly
- **Hun er en utrolig smuk ung kvinde.**
  She is an incredibly beautiful young woman.

553. **tjeneste** *nc* service, favor, duty
- **Kan du gøre mig en tjeneste?**
  Can you do me a favor?

554. **bog** *nc* book
- **Han skrev en bog inden han døde.**
  He wrote a book before he died.

555. **ende** *nc* end, finish
- **Vi bor for enden af gaden.**
  We live at the end of the street.

556. **ende** *v* to end, finish
- **Åh Gud, håber det ender godt.**
  Oh God, I hope it ends well.

557. **tal** *nn* number, figure, digit
- **Tallet er højere for mænd end for kvinder.**
  The number is higher for men than women.

558. **indenfor** *adv* indoors, inside
- **Vejret dårligt. Bliv indenfor.**
  The weather is bad. Stay inside.

559. **tillykke** *int* congratulations
- **Tillykke med dit bryllup.**
   Congratulations on your wedding.

560. **tv** *nn* TV
- **Må ikke se for meget TV.**
   Don't watch too much TV.

561. **mente** *v* meant (past tense of **mene**)
- **Jeg mente det ikke.**
   I didn't mean it.

562. **smule** *nc* little bit (of something)
- **Dette er en lille smule bedre.**
   This is a little bit better.

563. **dårlig** *adj* bad
- **Vejret er dårligt i dag.**
   The weather is bad today.

564. **skød** *v* shot (past tense of **skyde**)
- **Jeg så, at han skød hende.**
   I saw that he shot her.

565. **sendt** *v* sent (past participle of **sende**)
- **Hvornår blev pakken sendt?**
   When was the package sent?

566. **doktor** *nc* doctor
- **Jeg har brug for at se doktor Andersen.**
   I need to go see doctor Andersen.

567. **mangle** *v* to lack, be missing
- **Mangler min frakke.**
   My coat is missing.

568. **læse** *v* to read
- **Min far læser stadig avisen.**
   My father still reads the newspaper.

569. **vejr** *nn* weather
- **I morgen bliver vejret godt.**
  Tomorrow the weather will be good.

570. **makker** *nc* partner (sports), buddy, pal
- **Min tennis makker er værre end mig.**
  My tennis partner is worse than me.

571. **kaffe** *nc* coffee
- **Hvordan drikker du din kaffe?**
  How do you drink your coffee?

572. **enhver** *pro* every, each
- **Det kan enhver forstå.**
  Everyone can understand.

573. **otte** *num* eight
- **En blæksprutte har otte ben.**
  An octopus has eight legs.

574. **onkel** *nc* uncle
- **Min onkel bor i Aarhus.**
  My uncle lives in Aarhus.

575. **hår** *nn* hair
- **Hun har langt hår.**
  She has long hair.

576. **større** *adj* larger, bigger, greater
- **Din hund er større end min kat.**
  Your dog is bigger than my cat.

577. **præsident** *nc* president
- **Trump blev valgt til præsident.**
  Trump was elected president.

578. **beskytte** *v* to protect
- **Politiet formodes at beskytte folk.**
  The police are supposed to protect people.

579. **kigge** *v* to look
- **Hvem kigger du på?**
  Who are you looking at?

580. **fortsætte** *v* to go on, resume, persist
- **Anders fortsætter det samme job.**
  Anders is continuing the same job.

581. **fru** *nc* Mrs.
- **Godmorgen fru Hansen.**
  Good morning Mrs. Hansen.

582. **vild** *adj* wild, fierce, savage (**fare vild** - to get lost)
- **Er vi faret vild?**
  Are we lost?

583. **åbne** *v* to open
- **Butikken åbner klokken otte.**
  The store opens at eight o'clock.

584. **dyr** *nn* animal
- **Elefanter er store dyr.**
  Elephants are large animals.

585. **dyr** *adj* expensive
- **Danmark er et dyrt land.**
  Denmark is an expensive country.

586. **skade** *nc* damage, harm
- **Jeg ønsker ikke at skade dig.**
  I do not want to hurt you.

587. **billede** *nn* picture, photo
- **Jeg har billeder af mine børn.**
  I have photos of my children.

588. **syg** *adj* sick
- **Mine børn er altid syge.**
  My kids are always sick.

589. **sort** *adj* black
- **Jeg drikker sort kaffe.**
  I drink black coffee.

590. **bord** nn table, desk
- **Hvad er der på bordet?**
  What is on the table?

591. **højt** *adv* loudly
- **Hun græder meget højt.**
  She is crying very loudly.

592. **slået** *v* beaten (past participle of **slå**)
- **Deres klub har slået os 3-1.**
  Their club has beaten us 3-1.

593. **fest** *nc* party, celebration
- **Hvem kommer til din fest?**
  Who is coming to your party?

594. **sende** *v* to send
- **Jeg vil sende dig dokumentet i morgen.**
  I will send you that document tomorrow.

595. **lod** *v* let, left, allowed (past tense of **lade**)
- **Du lod vinduet stå åbent.**
  You left the window open.

596. **lig** *adj* similar, the same, identical
- **Denne kampagne er meget lig den fra sidste år.**
  This campaign is very similar to the one from last year.

597. **mistet** *v* lost (past participle of **miste**)
- **Han har mistet alle sine penge.**
  He has lost all of his money.

598. **røvhul** *nn* (vulgar) asshole
- **Jeg kender ham. Han er et rigtigt røvhul.**
  I know him. He is a real asshole.

599. **sex** *nc* sex
- **De er dating, men de har ikke haft sex.**
  They are dating but they haven't had sex.

600. **hertil** *adv* up to here
- **Det krævede hårdt arbejde at komme hertil.**
  It took hard work to get here.

601. **ære** *nc* honor
- **Familiens ære er på spil.**
  The family's honor is at stake.

602. **ære** *v* to honor
- **Vi vil ære hendes minde.**
  We will honor her memory.

603. **dame** *nc* lady, woman
- **En gammel dame bor i det hus.**
  An old lady lives in that house.

604. **fængsel** *nn* prison
- **Han tilbragte fem år i fængsel.**
  He spent five years in prison.

605. **lede** *v* to look, search
- **Jeg leder efter mine sko.**
  I am looking for my shoes.

606. **sat** *v* put, placed (past participle of **sætte**)
- **Vi har alle sat vores lid til dig.**
  We have all put our trust in you.

607. **anderledes** *adj* different
- **Er dette hus anderledes?**
  Is this house different?

608. **mester** *nc* champion, master
- **Hun er en berømt dansk mester.**
  She is a famous Danish champion.

609. **kontor** *nn* office
- **Hun arbejder i et stort kontor.**
  She works in a large office.

610. **sendte** *v* sent (past tense of **sende**)
- **Hun sendte mig et kort i sidste uge.**
  She sent me a card last week.

611. **drikke** *v* to drink
- **Jeg er tørstig. Jeg ønsker at drikke noget saft.**
  I am thirsty. I want to drink some juice.

612. **travl** *adj* busy
- **Jeg ved du har travlt.**
  I know you are busy.

613. **glemt** *v* forgotten (past participle of **glemme**)
- **Undskyld. Jeg har glemt dit navn.**
  I'm sorry. I have forgotten your name.

614. **skole** *nc* school
- **Min datter starter skole i år.**
  My daughter starts school this year.

615. **røre** *v* to move
- **Hun rørte ved min hånd.**
  She touched my hand.

616. **betjent** *nc* cop, police officer
- **Jeg har lige snakket med en af de lokale betjente.**
  I just talked to one of the local cops.

617. **forklare** *v* to explain
- **Kan du forklare denne sætning for mig?**
  Can you explain this sentence to me?

618. **umuligt** *adj* impossible
- **Det er umuligt at gøre.**
  That is impossible to do.

619. **herinde** *adv* in here
- **Der er for mange bier herinde**
  There are too many bees in here.

620. **drøm** *nc* dream
- **Jeg havde en mærkelig drøm i nat.**
  I had a strange dream last night.

621. **åben** *adj* open
- **Det er ok at sove med åbent vindue om natten.**
  It is okay to sleep with the window open at night.

622. **alting** *pro* everything
- **Alting er komplet.**
  Everything is complete.

623. **ene** *adj* alone, lonely
- **Han er alene i det nye land, men ikke ensom.**
  He is alone in the new country, but not lonely.

624. **meter** *nc* meter
- **Han er næsten to meter høj.**
  He is almost two meters tall.

625. **venlig** *adj* friendly
- **Hendes lærer er meget venlig.**
  Her teacher is very friendly.

626. **luft** *nc* air
- **Luften er så klar.**
  The air is so clear.

627. **tør** *adj* dry
- **Om vinteren er det meget tørt.**
  In the winter it is very dry.

628. **fange** *nc* prisoner
- **Skrev hun en bog om at være fange af kærligheden?**
  Did she write a book about being prisoner of love?

629. **fange** *v* to catch, capture
- **Jeg kan fange fisk.**
  I can catch fish.

630. **overhovedet** *adv* at all
- **Det generede mig slet ikke.**
  It didn't bother me at all.

631. **forhold** *nn* relationship
- **Deres forhold er i øjeblikket vanskeligt.**
  Their relationship is currently difficult.

632. **råd** *nn* advice
- **Du har brug for nogen til at give dig gode råd.**
  You need someone to give you good advice.

633. **frue** *nc* ma'am, lady
- **Undskyld frue.**
  Excuse me ma'am.

634. **uanset** *prep* regardless
- **Uanset vejret så går jeg en tur i parken klokken 8 om morgenen.**
  Regardless of the weather, I go for a walk in the park at 8 am.

635. **stole** *v* to rely on, depend on (**stole på**)
- **Du kan stole på mig.**
  You can rely on me.

636. **født** *v* born (past tense of **føde**)
- **Jeg er født i 1978.**
  I was born in 1978.

637. **forsigtigt** *adv* cautiously, carefully
- **Det er vigtigt at køre forsigtigt.**
  It is important to drive carefully.

638. **spurgte** *v* asked (past tense of **spørge**)
- **Du spurgte ikke mig.**
  You didn't ask me.

639. **netop** *adv* just, exactly, precisely
- **Vi skrev en sms til hinanden på nøjagtig samme tidspunkt.**
  We wrote a text to each other at exactly the same time.

640. **syntes** *v* seemed, appeared (past tense of **synes**)
- **Hun så ud til at have det fint.**
  She seemed fine.

641. **bekymret** *adj* worried
- **Din mor bliver bekymret, hvis du kommer for sent.**
  Your mom will be worried if you are late.

642. **falde** *v* to fall
- **Fra flyveren var der langt at falde.**
  From the plane there was a long way to fall.

643. **stil** *nc* style, manner
- **Min datter har sin egen stil.**
  My daughter has her own style.

644. **føles** *v* to feel, have feelings
- **Kan du forestille hvordan det må føles?**
  Can you imagine how it must fee?

645. **fare** *nc* danger, threat, hazard
- **Der er en fare for, at mange af disse familier vil sulte.**
  There is a danger that many of these families will go hungry.

646. **vende** *v* to turn
- **Vend dig og se på mig.**
  Turn around and look at me.

647. **forlade** *v* to leave
- **Ingen forlader lokalet.**
  No one leaves the room.

648. **dele** *v* to divide, share, split
- **Du er nødt til at dele dit legetøj med din bror.**
  You have to share your toys with your brother.

649. **tidspunkt** *nn* time, moment
- **Jeg var der på et tidspunkt i fortiden.**
  I was there at some time in the past.

650. **advokat** *nc* lawyer
- **Jeg er nødt til at ringe til min advokat.**
  I need to call my lawyer.

651. **halv** *adj* half
- **Det vil tage en halv time.**
  It will take half an hour.

652. **kendt** *v* known (past participle of **kende**)
- **Jeg har kendt ham i årevis.**
  I have known him for years.

653. **mødt** *v* met (past participle of **møde**)
- **Han har mødt alle på kontoret.**
  He has met everyone in the office.

654. **forelske** *v* to fall in love with
- **Jeg blev forelsket i en anden kvinde.**
  I fell in love with another woman.

655. **lærer** *nc* teacher
- **Jeg har en stor dansk lærer.**
  I have a great Danish teacher.

656. **slås** *v* to fight
- **Hun slås ofte med sin bror.**
  She fights often with her brother.

657. **stolt** *adj* proud
- **Amerikanerne er meget stolt folk.**
  Americans are very proud people.

658. **læge** *nc* doctor, physician
- **Jeg har en aftale med lægen.**
  I have an appointment with the doctor.

659. **mund** *nc* mouth
- **Han har en stor mund.**
  He has a big mouth.

660. **drink** *nc* drink (mixed alcoholic beverage)
- **Jeg har brug for en drink!**
  I need a drink!

661. **direkte** *adj* direct, immediate
- **I Danmark har de direkte valg.**
  In Denmark they have direct elections.

662. **mord** *nn* murder
- **Der skete et mord i byen i aftes.**
  There was a murder in the city last night.

663. **ændre** *v* to change
- **Dette vil ændre landet.**
  This will change the country.

664. **nemlig** *adv* namely, in fact, actually
- **Vi har samme mål, nemlig flere billige boliger.**
  We have the same goal, namely more affordable housing.

665. **telefon** *nc* telephone
- **Du har et opkald på telefonen.**
  You have a call on the telephone.

666. **angreb** *nn* attack
- **Statsministeren er under angreb.**
  The prime minister is under attack.

667. **ordre** *nc* order, command
- **Jeg tror, han ikke ved, hvordan man følger ordrer.**
  I don't think he knows how to follow orders.

668. **sikre** *v* to secure, ensure
- **Vi har arbejdet på at forsøge at sikre, at dette sker.**
  We have been working to try to ensure that happens.

669. **normalt** *adv* normally
- **Hun er normalt meget høflig.**
  She is normally very polite.

670. **konge** *nc* king
- **Frederik IX var konge af Danmark.**
  Frederik IX was the king of Denmark.

671. **ægte** *adj* true, right
- **Jeg håber at finde det ægte Danmark.**
  I hope to find the real Denmark.

672. **flyve** *v* to fly
- **Det tager tre timer at flyve derhen.**
  It takes three hours to fly there.

673. **ordne** *v* to order, sort out, arrange, tidy up
- **Før jeg kunne komme ind i landet måtte jeg ordne mine papirer.**
  Before I could enter the country I had to sort out my papers.

674. **ni** *num* nine
- **Jeg er på ferie i ni dage.**
  I am on vacation for nine days.

675. **rent** *adv* purely
- **Dette er ikke et rent akademisk spørgsmål.**
  This is not a purely academic question.

676. **ødelægge** *v* to destroy, ruin
- **Jordskælvet ødelagde bygningen.**
  The earthquake destroyed the building.

677. **skib** *nn* ship, boat
- **Vi rejste med skib.**
  We traveled by ship.

678. **satan** *nc* Satan, (vulgar) bastard, shit
- **Tror du på Satan?**
  Do you believe in Satan?

679. **fart** *nc* speed
- **Bilen kørte med høj fart.**
  The car was traveling at high speed.

680. **kontakt** *nc* contact, a contact person
- **Vi er i øjeblikket i kontakt med deres repræsentanter.**
  We are currently in contact with their representatives.

681. **gave** *nc* gift, present
- **Jeg er nødt til at købe en dejlig gave til min søster.**
  I have to buy a nice present for my sister.

682. **skør** *adj* insane, crazy
- **Han handler virkelig skørt.**
  He is acting really crazy.

683. **mødte** *v* met (past tense of **møde**)
- **De mødtes et par gange om året.**
  They met a few times per year.

684. **skrev** *v* wrote (past tense of **skrive**)
- **Hvem skrev den bog.**
  Who wrote that book.

685. **bestemt** *adj* particular, certain
- **Du er nødt til at følge disse instruktioner på en bestemt måde.**
  You have to follow these instructions in a certain way.

686. **ild** *nc* fire
- **Han satte ved et uheld ild til sit hus.**
  He accidently set fire to his house.

687. **middag** *nc* midday, noon, dinner
- **Hvornår vil du gerne spise middag?**
  When would you like to eat dinner?

688. **ryge** *v* to smoke
- **Hvornår begyndte du at ryge?**
  When did you start smoking?

689. **naturligvis** *adv* of course, naturally
- **Naturligvis er jeg ked af det.**
  Of course I am upset.

690. **stemme** *nc* voice
- **Hun har en meget høj stemme.**
  She has a very loud voice.

691. **slem** *adj* bad, serious
- **Sophie har et slemt tilfælde af influenza.**
  Sophie has a serious case of the flu.

692. **stand** *nc* position, social status, class, rank, occupation
- **Vi er ikke i stand til at reagere på dette tidspunkt.**
  We are not in a position to respond at this time.

693. **lukket** *nc* closed (past participle of **lukke**)
- **Hun har lukket sagen.**
  She has shut the case.

694. **skid** *nc* (vulgar) shit, damn
- **Der var ikke en skid.**
  There wasn't a damn thing.

695. **hav** *nn* sea, ocean
- **Jeg foretrækker at bo tæt på havet.**
  I prefer to live close to the sea.

696. **forsøge** *v* to try, attempt
- **Jeg vil forsøge at sende e-mailen igen.**
  I will try to send the email again.

697. **aftes** *nc* last night (**i aftes**)
- **Hvad tid faldt du i søvn i aftes?**
  What time did you go to sleep last night?

698. **jesus** *nc* Jesus, (mild swear)
- **Tror du på Jesus?**
  Do you believe in Jesus?

699. **blå** *adj* blue
- **Havet er blåt.**
  The ocean is blue.

700. **krop** *nc* body, torso
- **Hun har fire tatoveringer på sin krop.**
  She has four tattoos on her body.

701. **flytte** *v* to move
- **Han forsøger at flytte skrivebordet.**
  He is trying to move the desk.

702. **pæn** *adj* nice, nice-looking
- **Jeg mødte en meget søde kvinde.**
  I met a very good looking woman.

703. **pris** *nc* price
- **Prisen på huse er steget for meget.**
  The price of houses has risen too much.

704. **mistede** *v* lost (past tense of **miste**)
- **Jeg mistede min tegnebog igen.**
  I lost my wallet again.

705. **glemte** *v* forgot (past tense of **glemme**)
- **Desværre glemte jeg min vens fødselsdag.**
  Unfortunately I forgot my friend's birthday.

706. **forsvind** *int* go away, get lost
- **Gå!, Forsvind!**
  Get out!, Go away!

707. **stærk** *adj* strong
- **Hun er en meget stærk kvinde.**
  She is a very strong woman.

708. **hurtigere** *adj* faster
- **Din bil er nyere, men min er stadig hurtigere end din.**
  Your car is newer but mine is still faster than yours.

709. **starte** *v* to start up, to start
- **Når det er meget koldt vil min bil ikke starte.**
  When it is very cold my car won't start.

710. **nær** *adj* near, close
- **De bor i en lille by nær Aarhus.**
  They live in a small town near Aarhus.

711. **tabe** *nc* to lose
- **Nogle vil tabe mere end andre.**
  Some will lose more than others.

712. **undskylde** *v* to excuse, apologize
- **Jeg vil ikke undskylde for denne fremgangsmåde.**
  I will not apologize for this approach.

713. **frøken** *nc* miss
- **Farvel frøken Nielsen.**
  Goodbye Miss Nielsen.

714. **levende** *adj* alive, live
- **Eksporterer Danmark levende kvæg?**
  Does Denmark export live cattle?

715. **bryde** *v* to break
- **De bryder reglerne.**
  They are breaking the rules.

716. **derovre** *adv* over there
- **Hvad laver de derovre?**
  What are they doing over there?

717. **løgn** *nc* lie (untruth)
- **Hun fortalte mig en løgn, men jeg troede hende ikke.**
  She told me a lie but I didn't believe her.

718. **lært** *v* taught (past participle of **lære**)
- **Hun har lært mange studerende dansk.**
  She has taught Danish to many students.

719. **skrevet** *v* written (past participle of **skrive**)
- **Hvor mange bøger har han skrevet?**
  How many books has he written?

720. **magt** *nc* force, power
- **Efter at have fået magten ville han ikke slippe den.**
  After gaining power he wouldn't let it go.

721. **ro** *nc* calmness, rest, calm
- **Efter denne situation ser vi frem til politisk ro.**
  After that situation we are looking for political calm.

722. **underlig** *adv* odd, peculiar, strange
- **Han er en fin fyr, men han er en smule underlig.**
  He is a nice guy but he is a bit odd.

723. **løs** *adj* loose
- **Jeg har tabt mig og nu er min skjorte løs.**
  I have lost weight and now my shirt is loose.

724. **selvom** *conj* although, even though, in spite of
- **Men selvom de begge er gode, er den ene bedre.**
  Although they both are good, this one is better.

725. **enkelt** *adj* individual, single
- **Vores hold er kun et enkelt point efter det førende.**
  Our team is only a single point behind first place.

726. **sang** *v* sang (past tense of **synge**)
- **Hun sang smukt på karaoke i aftes.**
  She sang beautifully at karaoke last night.

727. **sang** nc song
- **Hvad er din favorit sang?**
  What is your favorite song?

728. **vred** *adj* angry
- **Min far er meget vred på mig.**
  My father is very angry at me.

729. **øl** *nn* beer
- **To øl tak.**
  Two beers please.

730. **rum** *nn* space, room
- **Astronauter rejse til det ydre rum.**
  Astronauts travel to outer space.

731. **lyve** *v* to lie (tell untruth)
- **Vær forsigtig. Han lyver.**
  Be careful. He lies.

732. **sulten** *adj* hungry
- **Kan vi spiser snart? Jeg er sulten.**
  Can we eat soon. I'm hungry.

733. **tredje** *num* third
- **Det var hans tredje scoring i sæsonen.**
  That was his third goal of the season.

734. **musik** *nc* music
- **Jeg elsker at lytte til musik.**
  I love to listen to music.

735. **parat** *adj* ready, prepared
- **Regeringen er parat til at bruge flere penge i år.**
  The government is prepared to spend more money this year.

736. **løjtnant** *nc* lieutenant
- **Andersen er løjtnant.**
  Andersen in the lieutenant.

737. **interessant** *adj* interesting
- **Filmen var meget interessant.**
  The movie was very interesting.

738. **midt** *nc* middle
- **Butikken er midt i byen.**
  The shop is in the middle of the town.

739. **miste** *v* to lose (something)
- **Denne gang kan jeg ikke miste mine nøgler.**
  This time I can't lose my keys.

740. **kammerat** *nc* buddy, mate, pal
- **Mandag spiste jeg frokost med en kammerat.**
  On Monday I ate dinner with a buddy.

741. **opgave** *nc* task
- **Vores opgave er at afslutte hurtigt.**
  Our task is to finish quickly.

742. **professor** *nc* professor
- **Hvem er din professor for denne klasse?**
  Who is your professor for that class?

743. **onde** *nn* evil
- **Kender du forskel på godt og ondt?**
  Do you know the difference between good and evil?

744. **hospital** *nn* hospital
- **Min bedstemor er på hospitalet.**
  My grandmother is in the hospital.

745. **ride** *v* to ride
- **Kan jeg ride på din hest?**
  Can I ride your horse?

746. **lægge** *v* to lay, put, place
- **Lægge blomsten på bordet.**
  Put the flower on the table.

747. **bevise** *v* to prove
- **Jeg ved, det er sandt, men jeg kan ikke bevise det.**
  I know it is true but I can't prove it.

748. **heldig** *adj* lucky, fortunate
- **Men kan vi blive ved med at være så heldige?**
  But can we continue to be so lucky?

749. **sur** *adj* angry, grouchy, sour
- **Det er derfor, jeg er så sur.**
  This is why I am so angry.

750. **sad** *v* sat (past tense of **sidde**)
- **Jeg sad på noget.**
  I sat on something.

751. **stjal** *v* stole (past tense of **stjæle**)
- **Nogen stjal mit ID-kort.**
  Someone stole my ID card.

752. **skam** *nc* shame, pity
- **Det er en skam den måde, de opfører sig.**
  It is a shame the way they are behaving.

753. **kraft** *nc* force, strength
- **Mangfoldighed er vores kraft.**
  Diversity is our strength.

754. **tidligt** *adv* early
- **Jeg er nødt til at vågne tidligt hver dag.**
  I have to wake up early every morning.

755. **savne** *v* to miss (feel the absence of)
- **Når jeg er væk hjemmefra, savner jeg min familie.**
  When I am away from home I miss my family.

756. **styrke** *v* to strengthen
- **Vi skal styrke vores lands konkurrenceevne.**
  We must strengthen our country's competitiveness.

757. **egentlig** *adj* real, actual, proper
- **Vi er ved at opbygge en egentlig mur.**
  We are building an actual wall.

758. **egentlig** *adv* after all, anyways
- **Så hvad er problemet egentlig?**
  So what is the problem anyway?

759. **danse** *v* to dance
- **Hun elsker virkelig at danse.**
  She really loves to dance.

760. **pludselig** *adj* sudden
- **Pludselig hører hun et barn, der græder.**
  Suddenly she hears a child crying.

761. **fjols** *nn* fool
- **Lyt ikke til ham, han er et fjols.**
  Don't listen to him, he is a fool.

762. **lege** *v* to play
- **Børnene leger pænt sammen.**
  The kids are playing nicely together.

763. **fremtid** *nc* future
- **Jeg ved ikke, hvad der vil ske i fremtiden.**
  I don't know what will happen in the future.

764. **tusind** *num* thousand
- **Tusind tak!**
  Thank a bunch (Thousand thanks)!

765. **kaldte** *v* called (past tense of **kalde**)
- **Hun kaldte hans præstation "en katastrofe".**
  She called his performance "a disaster".

766. **stol** *nc* chair
- **Sid på den stol.**
  Sit on that chair.

767. **hær** *nc* army
- **Den amerikanske hær er meget kraftfuld.**
  The American army is very powerful.

768. **ren** *adj* clean
- **Mit værelse er aldrig rent.**
  My room is never clean.

769. **læst** *nc* read (past participle of **læse**)
- **Har du læst nyhederne i dag.**
  Have you read the news today?

770. **mål** *nn* aim, goal, target
- **Forenkling er et vigtigt mål.**
  Simplification is an important goal.

771. **nyheder** *nc* news (plural)
- **Min kone elsker at læse nyheder.**
  My wife loves to read the news.

772. **lejlighed** *nc* apartment
- **Lad os gå til vores lejlighed.**
  Let's go to our apartment.

773. **kræve** *v* to demand, require
- **Arbejderne bør kræve en lønforhøjelse.**
  The workers should demand a raise.

774. **sko** *nc* shoe
- **Hvor mange nye sko har du købt?**
  How many new shoes did you buy?

775. **respekt** *nc* respect
- **Behandl andre mennesker med respekt.**
  Treat other people with respect.

776. **nem** *adj* easy
- **I øjeblikket er situationen bestemt ikke nem.**
  The situation at this moment is definitely not a simple one.

777. **både** *conj* both
- **Han havde både en bil og en motorcykel.**
  He had both a motorcycle and a car.

778. **ejer** *nc* owner
- **De har talt med ejeren.**
  They have spoken with the owner.

779. **tegn** *nn* sign
- **Det er ikke et tegn på fremskridt, men et tegn på vanvid.**
  It is not a sign of progress, but a sign of madness.

780. **kontrol** *nc* control
- **Jeg har altid brug for at føle mig i kontrol.**
  I always need to feel in control.

781. **gade** *nc* street
- **Hvilken gade voksede du op i?**
  What street did you grow up on?

782. **overalt** *adv* everywhere
- **Overalt i Danmark er folk flinke.**
  Everywhere in Denmark the people are nice.

783. **lærte** *v* taught (past tense of **lære**)
- **Hun lærte mig alt, hvad jeg ved.**
  She taught me everything I know.

784. **ganske** *adv* quite
- **Jeg skal gøre det ganske kort.**
  I'll make it (quite) brief.

785. **himmel** *nc* sky
- **Det kom som et lyn fra en klar himmel.**
  It was like a bolt from the clear blue sky.

786. **viste** *v* showed (past tense of **vise**)
- **Dette viste os, at det var muligt.**
  This showed us that it was possible.

787. **sjæl** *nc* soul
- **Han solgte sin sjæl til djævlen.**
  He sold his soul to the devil.

788. **fin** *adj* fine, good
- **Det er en fin service til en rimelig pris.**
  It is an excellent service at a reasonable price.

789. høj *adj* high, tall, loud
- **Denne opgave har høj prioritet.**
  This assignment is a high priority.

790. skæbne *nc* destiny, fate
- **Jeg mener, at Europa har en skæbne.**
  I believe that Europe has a destiny.

791. lav *adj* low, short (for people)
- **Min mor er meget lav.**
  My mother is very short.

792. brød *nn* bread
- **Min mor bager hjemmebagt brød.**
  My mother makes homemade bread.

793. kys *nn* kiss
- **Giv mig et kys.**
  Give me a kiss.

794. følelse *nc* feeling
- **Jeg har denne usikre følelse.**
  I have this insecure feeling.

795. særlig *adj* particularly, especially
- **Den økonomiske vækst er svag, særlig i Amerika.**
  Economic growth is weak, especially in America.

796. ødelagt *adj* damaged, destroyed
- **Huset blev ødelagt i stormen.**
  The house was damaged in the storm.

797. hul *nn* hole
- **Der er et hul i min indkørsel.**
  There is a hole in my driveway.

798. fisk *nc* fish
- **Spiser danskere mange fisk?**
  Do Danish people eat a lot of fish?

799. **håb** *nn* hope
- **Der er håb om, at dette år vil blive bedre.**
  There is hope that this year will be better.

800. **bringe** *v* to bring
- **Der er ingen grund til at bringe noget.**
  There is no need to bring anything.

801. **vor** *pro* (formal) our, ours
- **Der er en kirke i København kaldet "Vor Frue Kirke".**
  There is a church in Copenhagen called "Church of Our Lady".

802. **frygt** *nc* fear, fright
- **Terrorisme er først og fremmest frygt.**
  Terrorism is essentially about fear.

803. **søge** *v* to search, seek, look for
- **Folk er tvunget til at søge længere væk for at finde fisk.**
  People are forced to look further afield to find fish.

804. **sten** *nc* stone
- **Der er en massiv sten i vores have.**
  There is a massive stone in our garden.

805. **alvorligt** *adv* seriously
- **Vi tager disse trusler meget alvorligt.**
  We are taking these threats very seriously.

806. **drømme** *v* to dream
- **Man kan altid drømme om en bedre verden.**
  You can always dream of a better world.

807. **tjekke** *v* to check
- **Hvis du ikke kan finde e-mailen kan du tjekke din junk mail.**
  If you can't find the e-mail, you can check your junk mail folder.

808. **evigt** *adj* eternal, forever
- **Man må imidlertid også forstå, at intet varer evigt.**
  But we must also understand that nothing lasts forever.

809. **hvilke** *pro* what, which, who whom (plural of **hvilken**)
- **Hvilke lande vinder og hvilke lande taber?**
  Which countries will gain and which countries will lose?

810. **interesseret** *adj* interested
- **Jeg er interesseret i skandinavisk historie.**
  I am interested in Scandinavian history.

811. **bekymre** *v* to worry
- **Jeg ønsker ikke at mine forældre skal bekymre sig.**
  I don't want my parents to worry.

812. **medmindre** *adv* unless, except
- **Vi kan ikke afslutte medmindre alle arbejder hårdt.**
  We cannot finish unless everyone works hard.

813. **mulighed** *nc* opportunity, possibility, option
- **I år har jeg ikke mulighed for at tage til Danmark.**
  This year I don't have the opportunity to go to Denmark.

814. **satte** *v* set, put (past tense of **sætte**)
- **Hun satte sit glas på bordet.**
  She set her glass on the table.

815. **jul** *nc* Christmas
- **Jul i Danmark er smuk.**
  Christmas in Denmark is beautiful.

816. **adgang** *nc* access, admission
- **Museet har gratis adgang på tirsdage.**
  The museum has free admission on Tuesdays.

817. **dernede** *adv* down there
- **Er der stadig nogen der lever dernede?**
  Does anyone still live down there?

818. **fornøjelse** *nc* something pleasurable
- **Det er altid en fornøjelse at lytte til hende.**
  It is always a delight to listen to her.

819. **forsøgte** *v* tried (past tense of **forsøge**)
- **Vi forsøgte, men desværre var det ikke en succes.**
  We tried, but unfortunately weren't successful.

820. **hjerne** *nc* brain
- **Du bruger ikke kun 10 procent af din hjerne.**
  You do not only use 10 percent of your brain.

821. **vågne** *v* to wake up
- **Jeg er træt, jeg ønsker ikke at vågne endnu.**
  I am tired, I don't want to wake up yet.

822. **udmærket** *adj* excellent, superb
- **Det var en virkelig udmærket bog.**
  It was a truly excellent book.

823. **ens** *adj* identical, alike, equally
- **Det er væsentligt, at alle medarbejdere behandles ens.**
  It is essential that all employees are treated equally.

824. **ekstra** *adj* extra, additional
- **Det ekstra problem for os er vejret.**
  The added problem for us is the weather.

825. **rød** *adj* red
- **Kan du se den røde fugl?**
  Can you see the red bird?

826. **ærlig** *adj* honest, sincere
- **Politikere er ikke altid ærlige.**
  Politicians are not always honest.

827. **tjener** *nc* waiter, servant
- **Kan du kalder på tjeneren, tak.**
  Can you call the waiter over, thanks.

828. **pokker** *nc* (vulgar) Devil, Damn it
- **For pokker! Jeg slog min tå.**
  Damn it! I hit my toe.

829. **derfra** *adv* from there
- **Derfra er det en meget kort køretur til centrum.**

  From there it is a very short drive to downtown.

830. **personlig** *adj* personal
- **Jeg kan ikke fortælle dig, fordi det er personlige oplysninger.**

  I can't tell you because that is personal information.

831. **sælge** *v* to sell
- **Min tante sælger bøger.**

  My aunt sells books.

832. **is** *nc* ice
- **Ønsker du is i din drink?**

  Do you want ice in your drink?

833. **stakkels** *adj* poor, pitiful
- **Nårh, den stakkels lille hvalp!**

  Oh, that poor little puppy!

834. **dens** *pro* its (possessive of **den**)
- **Jeg ønsker ikke at tage dens mad væk.**

  I don't want to take its food away.

835. **minde** *nn* a memory
- **Det er vigtigt at ære deres minde.**

  It is important to honor their memory.

836. **dejlig** *adj* delightful, lovely, beautiful
- **Der er en meget dejlig sang, som vi ofte synger i vores familie.**

  There is a very lovely song that we often sing in our family.

837. **forlod** *v* left (past tense of **forlade**)
- **Han forlod hende, da de havde været gift i et år.**

  He left her, after they had been married for a year.

838. **hest** *nc* horse
- **Kan du ride en hest?**

  Can you ride a horse?

839. **enten** *conj* either (... or)
- **Du kan enten få kaffe eller the.**
  You can either have coffee or tea.

840. **tanke** *nc* thought, idea
- **Jeg har lige haft en interessant tanke.**
  I just had an interesting thought.

841. **dybt** *adv* deeply, extremely
- **Jeg var dybt forelsket i ham.**
  I was deeply in love with him.

842. **fod** *nc* foot
- **Min fod gør ondt.**
  My foot hurts.

843. **nervøs** *adj* nervous
- **Jeg bliver nervøs, når vi taler foran folk.**
  I get nervous talking in front of people.

844. **farlig** *adj* dangerous
- **Det kan være farligt at køre i et andet land.**
  It can be dangerous to drive in another country.

845. **lukke** *v* to close
- **Luk døren bag dig.**
  Close the door behind you.

846. **tænder** *nc* teeth
- **Hun har meget hvide tænder.**
  She has very white teeth.

847. **hurtig** *adj* quick, rapid, fast
- **Jeg hører en bil køre meget hurtigt.**
  I hear a car driving very quickly.

848. **hoppe** *nn* to jump
- **Det er så sjovt at hoppe i trampolin.**
  It is so much fun to jump on the trampoline.

849. **deroppe** *adv* up there
- **Der er en vidunderlig udsigt deroppe fra.**
  There is a wonderful view from up there.

850. **bære** *v* to carry
- **Jeg forsøgte at bære alt, men det var for tungt.**
  I tried to carry everything but it was too heavy.

851. **vandt** *v* won (past tense of **vinde**)
- **Vi tabte kampen, men vandt krigen.**
  We lost the battle but won the war.

852. **tabt** *adj* lost (past participle of **tabe**)
- **Har du tabt dig?**
  Have you lost weight?

853. **lå** *v* lay (past tense of **ligge**)
- **Hun lå på midten af vejen.**
  She lay down in the middle of the road.

854. **lagde** *v* laid, put, set (past tense of **lægge**)
- **Derefter tog han sin jakke og lagde den på jorden.**
  Then he took off his jacket and laid it on the ground.

855. **nødvendigt** *nc* necessary
- **Det kunne være sjovt, men det er ikke nødvendigt.**
  It might be fun but it's not necessary.

856. **enig** *adj* in agreement
- **Jeg er enig i, at tingene skal ændres.**
  I agree that things need to change.

857. **start** *nc* start
- **Det var en frygtelig start.**
  This was a terrible start.

858. **søvn** *nc* sleep
- **Jeg har brug for meget mere søvn for at være lykkelig.**
  I need a lot more sleep to be happy.

859. **fortjene** *v* to deserve
- **Dette parti fortjener ikke din stemme.**
  That party doesn't deserve your vote.

860. **morder** *nc* murderer
- **Politiet har endelig anholdt morderen.**
  The police have finally arrested the murderer.

861. **bagefter** *adv* behind, afterwards, subsequently
- **Bagefter kan man passende leje en cykel.**
  Afterwards you might want to rent a bike.

862. **område** *nn* area, space
- **Dette er et økologisk følsomt område.**
  This is an ecologically sensitive area.

863. **tilfælde** *nn* case, instance, accident
- **I nogle tilfælde er det næsten umuligt.**
  In some cases it is nearly impossible.

864. **vælge** *v* to choose
- **Jeg kan ikke vælge mellem to kvinder.**
  I can't choose between two women.

865. **hverken** *adv* neither (**hverken ... eller ...**)
- **Hverken Det Hvide Hus eller præsidenten vil kommentere sagen yderligere.**
  Neither the White House nor the president will comment further.

866. **båd** *nc* boat
- **De ville ikke engang gå ned i båden.**
  They would not even go out in the boat.

867. **sindssyg** *adj* insane, crazy
- **Det har gennem tiden gjort ham sindssyg.**
  It has over time made him crazy.

868. **minut** *nn* minute
- **Jeg ringer tilbage om et minut.**
  I will call you back in one minute.

869. **frokost** *nc* lunch (midday meal)
- **Jeg spiste en lækker sandwich til frokost.**
  I ate a delicious sandwich for lunch.

870. **love** *v* to promise
- **Jeg lover at elske dig for evigt.**
  I promise to love you forever.

871. **varm** *adj* warm, hot
- **Brasilien er et meget varmt land.**
  Brazil is a very hot country.

872. **glæde** *nc* joy, pleasure
- **Det er med stor glæde, at jeg inviterer dig.**
  It is with great pleasure that I invite you.

873. **glæde** *v* to look forward to (**glæde sig til**)
- **Jeg glæder mig til weekenden.**
  I am looking forward to the weekend.

874. **soldat** *nc* soldier
- **Han var soldat i den danske hær.**
  He was a soldier in the Danish army.

875. **gulv** *nn* floor
- **Jeg vil have et hus med smukke gulve.**
  I want a house with beautiful floors.

876. **forskellig** *adj* different
- **Dette er en helt forskellig situation denne gang.**
  This is a very different situation this time.

877. **ryg** *nc* back, spine
- **Han har en tatovering på ryggen.**
  He has a tattoo on his back.

878. **lytte** *v* to listen
- **Jeg fortæller altid min, at søn han skal lytte til mig.**
  I am always telling my son to listen to me.

879. **overleve** *v* to survive
- **Man kan ikke overleve uden mad og vand.**
  You can't survive without food and water.

880. **stjålet** *v* stolen (past participle of **stjæle**)
- **Vores kreditkort blev stjålet.**
  Our credit card was stolen.

881. **fuldstændig** *adv* completely
- **Du har fuldstændig misforstået.**
  You have completely misunderstood.

882. **fyldt** *adj* full
- **Jeg mener personligt, at glasset er halvt fyldt.**
  I personally believe that the glass is half full.

883. **forsvinde** *v* to vanish, disappear
- **Dine sko kan ikke bare forsvinde.**
  Your shoes can't just disappear.

884. **besøg** *nn* visit
- **Jeg kan kun holde til et kort besøg.**
  I can only stay for a short visit.

885. **hotel** *nn* hotel
- **Vi opholdt os på et fem-stjernet hotel.**
  We stayed in a five star hotel.

886. **stjæle** *v* to steal
- **De blev beskyldt for at stjæle deres konkurrents teknologi.**
  They were accused of stealing their competitor's technology.

887. **brænde** *v* to burn
- **Han blev anholdt for at brænde flaget.**
  He was arrested for burning the flag.

888. **takke** *v* to thank
- **Jeg vil gerne takke dig for dit hårde arbejde.**
  I want to thank you for your hard work.

889. **vagt** *nc* guard, watch
- **De blev oplyst om at være på vagt.**
  They were told to be on guard.

890. **højere** *adj* higher
- **Vi vil ikke have råd, hvis priserne bliver højere.**
  We won't be able to afford if prices go any higher.

891. **gruppe** *nc* group, unit, team
- **Vi havde en stort gruppe af ingeniører.**
  We had a large team of engineers.

892. **solen** *nc* the Sun
- **Planeterne kredser om Solen.**
  The planets orbit the Sun.

893. **bar** *nc* bar (place that serves drinks)
- **Han mødte sin kone på en bar**
  He met his wife in a bar.

894. **bar** *v* carried, bore (past tense of **bære**)
- **Han bar sin datter på ryggen.**
  He carried his daughter on his back.

895. **vilje** *nc* will (volition)
- **Desværre er der ingen større politisk vilje.**
  Unfortunately there is no more political will.

896. **dengang** *adv* back then, at that time
- **Dengang var det en stor restaurant.**
  At that time it was a large restaurant.

897. **lagt** *v* laid, put, set (past participle of **lægge**)
- **Hun har lagt sig for natten.**
  She had laid down for the night.

898. **ovre** *adj* over
- **Vinteren er ovre, så det er ikke så koldt.**
  Winter is over so it isn't as cold.

899. **korrekt** *adj* correct
- **Det er vigtigt, at alle vores beregninger er korrekte.**
  It is important that all of our calculations are correct.

900. **derefter** *adv* after that, afterwards
- **Derefter tilsættes olien til blandingen.**
  After that the oil is added to the mixture.

901. **gal** *adj* mad
- **Derfor var jeg så gal på Axel.**
  That is why I was so mad at Axel.

902. **nærhed** *nc* closeness, nearness
- **Vi bor alle i byen eller i nærheden.**
  We all live in the city or nearby.

903. **situation** *nc* situation
- **Detaljerne varierer fra situation til situation.**
  The details vary from situation to situation.

904. **forsøg** *nn* attempt, try, effort
- **Dette er et forsøg på at angribe statsministeren.**
  This is an attempt to attack the prime minister.

905. **sergent** *nc* sergeant
- **Han er sergent i det amerikanske militær.**
  He is a sergeant in the American military.

906. **smerte** *nc* pain, suffering
- **Jeg er bange for, at det vil forårsage smerte og lidelse.**
  I'm afraid this will cause pain and suffering.

907. **valgte** *v* chose (past tense of **vælge**)
- **Han valgte den sikreste løsning.**
  He chose the safest option.

908. **lækker** *adj* delicious
- **Min bedstemors mad er meget lækker.**
  My grandmother's food is very delicious.

909. **blandt** *prep* among
- **Han er blandt de bedste kokke i Danmark**
  He is among the best chefs in Denmark.

910. **klog** *adj* sensible, wise, intelligent
- **Jeg tror, det var en klog og fornuftig beslutning.**
  I believe it was a wise and sensible decision.

911. **glas** *nn* glass (substance), glass (drinking vessel)
- **Vil du gerne have et glas vand?**
  Would you like a glass of water.

912. **tilladelse** *nc* permission, authorization, licence, permit
- **Skal jeg have en tilladelse for at fælde et træ?**
  Do I need a permit to cut down a tree?

913. **købte** *v* bought (past tense of **købe**)
- **Jeg købte ikke nok mad til alle.**
  I didn't buy enough food for everyone.

914. **fjern** *adj* distant, remote
- **Min familie er flyttet til en fjern region.**
  My family has moved to a remote region.

915. **flod** *nc* river
- **Amazon er den længste flod i verden.**
  The Amazon is the longest river in the world.

916. **styre** *nn* government, regime, management
- **Styret har været ved magten for længe.**
  The regime has been in power for too long.

917. **styre** *v* to control, manage, govern
- **Kan du styre dine børn?**
  Can you control your children?

918. **forvente** *v* to expect
- **Hvornår kan vi forvente at se det endelige produkt?**
  When can we expect to see the final product.

919. **dreje** *v* to turn, revolve
   - **Hele verden drejer sig ikke om dig.**
     The whole world doesn't revolve around you.

920. **overfor** *adv* opposite
   - **Et nyt par flyttede ind i huset overfor.**
     A new couple moved in next door.

921. **slukke** *v* to put out, turn off
   - **Brandfolkene ankom for at slukke ilden.**
     The firefighters arrived to put out the fire.

922. **myrde** *v* to murder
   - **Han blev dømt for at have myrdet sin kone.**
     He was convicted of murdering his wife.

923. **selvmord** *nn* suicide
   - **Selvmord er et socialt problem.**
     Suicide is a social problem.

924. **lykkelig** *adj* happy, fortunate
   - **Hun er tryg og lykkelig.**
     She is confident and happy.

925. **jord** *nc* earth, dirt, soil, ground
   - **Der er forskellige kvaliteter af jord.**
     There are different qualities of soil.

926. **brev** *nn* letter
   - **Jeg har ikke modtaget et brev i lang tid.**
     I haven't received a letter in a long time.

927. **modtage** *v* to receive
   - **Vi var begejstrede for endelig at modtage vores gaver.**
     We were excited to finally receive our presents.

928. **bank** *nc* bank
   - **Mind mig om at gå i banken.**
     Remind me to go to the bank.

929. **ovenpå** *adv* on (the) top, upstairs
- **Han gik ovenpå til sit værelse.**
  He went upstairs to his room.

930. **tit** *adv* often, frequently
- **Det er ikke tit nok.**
  That is not often enough.

931. **kræfter** *nc* forces, strengths (plural of **kraft**)
- **Vi beskæftiger os med magtfulde kræfter.**
  We are dealing with powerful forces.

932. **stikker** *nc* informer, snitch
- **Den mand, der blev dræbt var en politi stikker.**
  The man who got killed was a police informer.

933. **gravid** *adj* pregnant
- **Tillykke! Jeg hørte du er gravid.**
  Congratulations! I heard you are pregnant.

934. **skifte** *nn* to change, exchange, swap
- **Jeg har brug for at skifte tøj.**
  I have to change my clothes.

935. **kød** *nn* meat
- **Hendes søster spiser ikke kød.**
  Her sister doesn't eat meat.

936. **morges** *adv* this morning (**i morges**)
- **Jeg var meget træt i morges.**
  I am very tired this morning.

937. **røg** *nc* smoke
- **Hvor der er røg er der ild.**
  If there is smoke there is fire.

938. **arm** *nc* arm
- **Desværre brækkede han armen.**
  Unfortunately he broke his arm.

939. **overraskelse** *nc* surprise
- **Nej, sikke en overraskelse!**
  Oh, What a surprise!

940. **fremad** *adj* forward, onward, ahead
- **Det er et stort skridt fremad for landet.**
  It is a big step forward for the country.

941. **træ** *nn* tree
- **Der er et stort træ i gården.**
  There is a big tree in the yard.

942. **tjene** *v* to earn (wage), make (money), profit
- **Hvor meget tjener en kirurg?**
  How much does a surgeon earn?

943. **mørk** adj dark
- **Da der var nogen måne, var natten meget mørk.**
  Since there was no moon the night was very dark.

944. **skabe** *v* to create
- **Dette vil skabe en ny mulighed for os.**
  This will create a new opportunity for us.

945. **især** *adv* especially
- **Tallet er højt, især blandt kvinder.**
  The number is high, especially among women.

946. **uheld** *nn* accident, mishap
- **Undskyld. Det var et uheld.**
  I'm sorry. It was an accident.

947. **gifte** *v* to marry
- **Han bad mig om at gifte mig med sig.**
  He asked me to marry him.

948. **vindue** *nn* window
- **Det er koldt. Luk vinduet.**
  It is cold. Close the window.

949. **herover** *adv* over here
- **Intet sker herover.**

  Nothing is happening over here.

950. **slag** *nn* blow, battle, beating
- **Dette har været et slag for vores økonomi.**

  This has been a blow to our economy.

951. **hænge** *v* to hang, hang up
- **Hun bad mig om at hænge billederne op i dag.**

  She asked me to hang up the pictures today.

952. **skat** *nc* tax, treasure
- **Præsidenten vil sænke skatter.**

  The president will lower taxes.

953. **klasse** *nc* class (group of students in a school)
- **Der er en ny elev i vores klasse.**

  There is a new student in our class.

954. **seriøst** *adv* serious
- **Jeg mener det seriøst!**

  I am serious, I mean it!

955. **gratis** *adj* free (no cost)
- **Er det gratis at parkere i weekenden?**

  Is it free to park on weekends?

956. **selskab** *nn* company, firm
- **Jeg arbejder for et stort dansk selskab.**

  I work for a large Danish company.

957. **brudt** *v* broken (past participle of **bryde**)
- **De har brudt deres forlovelse efter fire års forhold.**

  They have broken off their engagement after a four year relationship.

958. **tvivl** *nc* doubt
- **Hvis nogen skulle være i tvivl.**

  If anyone should be in doubt

959. **knap** *adv* hardly, scarcely, barely
- **Jeg var knap kommet hjem før barnet begyndte at græde.**
  I was barely home when the baby started crying.

960. **tilhøre** *v* to belong to
- **Denne tegnebog tilhører Jens.**
  That wallet belongs to Jens.

961. **frihed** *nc* freedom
- **De kæmpede for deres frihed.**
  They fought for their freedom.

962. **hemmelighed** *nc* secret
- **Kan du holde på en hemmelighed?**
  Can you keep a secret?

963. **fødselsdag** *nc* birthday
- **Vi holder en fest på vores datters fødselsdag.**
  We are having a party for our daughter's birthday.

964. **sørge** *v* to take care, see to, make sure
- **Sørg for at alt er i bilen.**
  Make sure everything is in the car.

965. **rig** *adj* rich
- **De er en rig familie.**
  They are a rich family.

966. **guld** *nn* gold
- **Hendes ring er af 24-karat guld.**
  Her ring is 24-karat gold.

967. **medicin** *nc* medicine
- **Du skal stoppe med din medicin for at få det bedre.**
  You must finish your medicine to get better.

968. **ø** *nc* island
- **København ligger på en ø.**
  Copenhagen is located in an island.

969. **løj** *v* lied, told untruth (past tense of **lyve**)
- **Vi har endelig fundet ud af, at han løj.**
  We finally found out that he lied.

970. **svare** *v* to answer, reply, respond
- **Kan du svare på min e-mail, så snart du kan?**
  Can you reply to my e-mail as soon as you can?

971. **ældre** *adj* older (comparative of **gammel**)
- **Deres hus er ældre end vores.**
  Their house is older than ours.

972. **grin** *nn* make fun of (**gøre grin af**)
- **Børnene i skolen gør grin af mig.**
  The kids at school make fun of me.

973. **undgå** *v* to evade, avoid
- **Dette selskab var et forsøg på at undgå at betale skat.**
  That company was trying to avoid paying taxes.

974. **vegne** *npl* behalf (**på vegne af** - on behalf of)
- **Jeg vil gerne takke dig på vegne af hele holdet.**
  I would like to thank you on behalf of the entire team.

975. **major** *nc* major (rank)
- **Han blev forfremmet. Han er major nu.**
  He was promoted. He is a major now.

976. **optaget** *adj* occupied, taken, busy
- **Dette emne har optaget meget tid.**
  This topic has occupied a lot of time.

977. **flygte** *v* to flee, escape, get away
- **Fangen forsøger at flygte.**
  The prisoner is trying to escape.

978. **spændende** *adj* exciting, suspenseful, gripping
- **Det er et spændende projekt for os.**
  This is an exciting project for us.

979. **sværd** *nn* sword
- **Ridderen kæmpede bravt med sit sværd.**
  The knight fought bravely with his sword.

980. **herude** *adv* out here
- **Hvorfor er du herude i kulden?**
  Why are you out here in the cold?

981. **forskel** *nc* difference
- **I teorien er der ingen forskel mellem teori og praksis.**
  In theory, there is no difference between theory and practice.

982. **låne** *v* to borrow, lend
- **Det er en dårlig idé at låne penge til en god ven.**
  It's a bad idea to lend money to a good friend.

983. **frisk** *adj* fresh
- **Denne fisk er ikke frisk.**
  This fish isn't fresh.

984. **fjerne** *v* to remove, to take off
- **Et af dens centrale mål er at fjerne amerikansk engagement.**
  One of its key aims is to remove American involvement.

985. **totalt** *adv* totally
- **Denne situation er totalt uacceptabel.**
  This situation is totally unacceptable.

986. **skridt** *nn* step, footstep
- **Derfor er det så vigtigt, at komme videre skridt for skridt.**
  This is why it is so important to proceed step by step.

987. **godaften** *int* good evening
- **Godaften og velkommen til vores hjem!**
  Good evening and welcome to our home!

988. **nærmere** *adj* nearer, closer
- **Ved nærmere eftersyn er det ikke så svært.**
  On closer inspection it is not that difficult.

989. **købt** *v* bought (past participle of **købe**)
- **Har du købt dine billetter?**
  Have you bought your tickets?

990. **kop** *nc* cup
- **En kop kaffe ville nok gøre godt!**
  A cup of coffee does seem like a good idea!

991. **koste** *v* to cost
- **Det vil koste dig flere penge, end du tror.**
  It will cost you more money than you think.

992. **langsomt** *adv* slowly
- **Folk er utålmodige, fordi det går så langsomt.**
  People are impatient because things are going so slowly.

993. **hyggelig** *adj* nice, friendly, cozy, comfortable
- **Vi bor i et lille, men hyggeligt hus.**
  We live in a small but cozy house.

994. **regel** *nc* rule
- **Læs alle reglerne grundigt.**
  Read all of the rules carefully.

995. **halvdelen** *nc* half
- **Halvdelen af dem er her ikke endnu.**
  Half of them aren't here yet.

996. **vælger** *nc* voter
- **Vælgerne er ikke tilfredse med kandidaterne.**
  The voters are not happy with the candidates.

997. **gemme** *v* to hide, conceal
- **Man skal ikke gemme sig bag en maske.**
  One should not hide behind a mask.

998. **beholde** *v* to keep, preserve
- **Jeg vil beholde mit gamle telefonnummer.**
  I want to keep my old phone number.

999. **ofte** *adv* often, frequently
  - **Vi hører ofte, at folk ikke har tillid til regeringen.**
    We often hear that people don't trust the government.

1000. **ferie** *nc* holiday, vacation
  - **Sidste år tog vi til Thailand på ferie.**
    Last year we went to Thailand on vacation.

1001. **dygtig** *adv* skilled, able
  - **Han er en meget dygtig pilot.**
    He is a highly skilled pilot.

ALPHABETICAL INDEX

brudt *v* broken 957
brug *nc* use, need 147
bruge *v* to use 213
bryde *v* to break 715
brænde *v* to burn 887
brød *nn* bread 792
burde *v* should, ought to 211
by *nc* city 429
bære *v* to carry 850
bør *v* should, ought to 427
børn *nn* children 262
båd *nc* boat 866
både *conj* both 777
chance *nc* chance 369
chef *nc* boss 494
da *conj* when, as, because 88
dag *nc* day 124
dame *nc* lady, woman 603
danse *v* to dance 759
datter *nc* daughter 389
de *art* the (pl), those 18
de *pro* they 19
dejlig *adj* delightful, lovely 836
del *nc* part, portion 308
dele *v* to divide, share, split 648
dem *pro* them 53
den *art* the (common), that 20
dengang *adv* back then 896
denne *pro* this, this one 120
dens *pro* its 834
der adv there 23
der *pro* who, which (relative) 24
derefter *adv* after that 900
deres *pro* their 112
derfor *adv* therefore 270
derfra *adv* from there 829
derinde *adv* in there 534
dernede *adv* down there 817
deroppe *adv* up there 849
derovre *adv* over there 716
derude *adv* out there 501
desværre *adv* unfortunately 549
det *pro* that, it 3

det *art* the (neuter) 4
dette *pro* this 117
dig *pro* you 27
din *pro* your, yours 50
direkte *adj* direct 661
disse *pro* these, these ones 240
dog *conj* though 339
doktor *nc* doctor 566
dreje *v* to turn, revolve 919
dreng *nc* boy 300
drikke *v* to drink 611
drink *nc* drink (alcoholic) 660
dræbe *v* to kill 299
drøm *nc* dream 620
drømme *v* to dream 806
du *pro* you 5
dum *adj* stupid, foolish 529
dybt *adv* deeply, extremely 841
dygtig *adv* skilled, able 1001
dyr *nn* animal 584
dyr *adj* expensive 585
dø *v* to die 260
død *adj* dead 179
død *nc* death 180
døde *v* died 226
dør *nc* door 304
dårlig *adj* bad 563
dårligt *adv* badly, poorly 528
efter *prep* after 85
egen *adj* own 346
egentlig *adj* real, actual 757
egentlig *adv* after all 758
ejer *nc* owner 778
ekstra *adj* extra, additional 824
eller *conj* or 77
ellers *adv* otherwise 249
elske *v* to love 166
elskede *nc* beloved 473
en *art* a, an (common) 9
én *num* one 284
end *conj* than 128
ende *nc* end, finish 555
ende *v* to end, finish 556

frem *adv* forward, toward 305
fremad *adj* forward ahead 940
fremtid *nc* future 763
fri *adj* free 362
frihed *nc* freedom 961
frisk *adj* fresh 983
frokost *nc* lunch 869
fru *nc* Mrs. 581
frue *nc* ma'am, lady 633
frygt *nc* fear, fright 802
frøken *nc* miss 713
fuld *adj* full 422
fuldstændig *adv* completely 881
fundet *adv* found 277
fyldt *adj* full 882
fyr *nc* guy, chap, bloke 229
fængsel *nn* prison 604
færdig *adj* finished 366
fødselsdag *nc* birthday 963
født *v* born 636
føle *v* to feel, touch 391
følelse *nc* feeling 794
føles *v* to feel 644
følge *v* to follow 539
før *prep* before 134
først *adv* at first, only 237
første *adj* first 195
få *v* to get, have 73
få *adj* few 74
fået *v* gotten, got 235
gade *nc* street 781
gal *adj* mad 901
galt *adv* wrong 269
gamle *adj* old (plural) 252
gammel *adj* old 363
gang *nc* time (occurrence) 136
gange *nc* times 273
ganske *adv* quite 784
gav *v* gave 266
gave *nc* gift, present 681
gemme *v* to hide, conceal 997
gennem *prep* through 357
gerne *adv* with pleasure 171

gide *v* to be bothered, care 545
gift *adj* married 416
gifte *v* to marry 947
gik *v* went 200
give *v* to give 173
gjorde *v* did 135
gjort *v* done 191
glad *adj* happy, glad 314
glas *nn* glass 911
glemme *v* to forget 400
glemt *v* forgotten 613
glemte *v* forgot 705
glæde *nc* joy, pleasure 872
glæde *v* to look forward to 873
god *adj* good 59
godaften *int* good evening 987
goddag *int* good day, hello 485
godmorgen *int* good morning 500
godnat *int* good night 507
gratis *adj* free (no cost) 955
gravid *adj* pregnant 933
grin *nn* make fun of 972
grund *nc* reason, cause 287
gruppe *nc* group, unit 891
gud *nc* god, (a mild curse) 156
guld *nn* gold 966
gulv *nn* floor 875
gut *nc* boy, guy, bloke 519
gøre *v* to do 62
gå *v* to go 82
gået *v* gone 328
hade *v* to hate 380
hallo *int* hello 255
halv *adj* half 651
halvdelen *nc* half 995
ham *pro* him 45
han *pro* he 28
hans *pro* his 98
har *v* has 11
hav *nn* sea, ocean 695
havde *v* had 84
have *v* to have 60

indenfor *adv* inside 558
indtil *conj* until 338
ingen *pro* no, nobody 79
ingenting *pro* nothing 326
interessant *adj* interesting 737
interesseret *adj* interested 810
intet *pro* nothing 178
is *nc* ice 832
især *adv* especially 945
ja *int* yes 41
jeg *pro* I 2
jer *pro* you (pl. obj.) 107
jeres *pro* your (plural) 184
jesus *nc* Jesus 698
jo *adv* after all, obviously 105
jo *int* yes 106
job *nn* job, work 359
jord *nc* earth, dirt, soil 925
jorden *nc* the Earth 404
jul *nc* Christmas 815
kaffe *nc* coffee 571
kalde *v* to call, refer to 358
kaldte *v* called 765
kammerat *nc* buddy, mate 740
kamp *nc* fight, battle 491
kan *v* can, be able 29
kaptajn *nc* captain 336
kede *v* to be bored 253
kende *v* to know 159
kendt *v* known 652
kendte *v* knew 542
kigge *v* to look 579
klar *adj* ready 161
klare *v* to manage, handle 298
klart *adv* clearly 504
klasse *nc* class 953
klog *adj* sensible, wise 910
klokken *nc* o'clock 437
knap *adv* hardly, barely 959
knægt *nc* boy, lad 446
kom *v* came 49
komme *v* to come 72
kone *nc* wife 276

konge *nc* king 670
kontakt *nc* contact 680
kontor *nn* office 609
kontrol *nc* control 780
kop *nc* cup (vessel) 990
korrekt *adj* correct 899
kort *adj* short, brief 410
koste *v* to cost 991
kraft *nc* force, strength 753
krig *nc* war 477
krop *nc* body, torso 700
kræfter *nc* forces, strengths 931
kræve *v* to demand 773
kun *adv* only 111
kunne *v* could, would 75
kvinde *nc* woman 296
kys *nn* kiss 793
kæft *nc* (vulgar) mouth 324
kæmpe *v* to fight, struggle 508
kære *adj* dear 441
kæreste *nc* boyfriend or girlfriend 444
kærlighed *nc* love 458
købe *v* to buy 537
købt *v* bought 989
købte *v* bought 913
kød *nn* meat 935
køre *v* to drive 315
kører *nc* driver 370
lade *v* to let, allow 66
lagde *v* laid, put, set 854
lagt *v* laid, put, set 897
land *nn* country 428
lang *adj* long (distance) 330
langsomt *adv* slowly 992
langt *adv* far 307
lav *adj* low, short 791
lave *v* to make, create, do 138
lede *v* to look, search 605
leder *nc* leader, manager 322
lege *v* to play 762
lejlighed *nc* apartment 772
let *adj* easy 521

leve *v* to live, be alive 398
levende *adj* alive 714
lide *v* to suffer 185
lidt *adj* a little, a bit 110
lig *adj* similar, identical 596
lige *adj* straight, even, just 63
ligeglad *adj* indifferent 511
ligesom *adv* sort of 257
ligge *v* to lie, to be 376
ligne *v* to resemble 371
lille *adj* small, little 144
liv *nn* life 157
lod *v* let, left, allowed 595
lort *nc* crap, shit (vulgar) 251
lov *nc* law 431
love *v* to promise 870
luft *nc* air 626
lukke *v* to close 845
lukket *nc* closed 693
lyd *nc* sound 333
lykke *nc* happiness, luck 497
lykkelig *adj* happy 924
lys *nn* light 546
lyst *nc* inclination, desire 475
lytte *v* to listen 878
lyve *v* to lie (tell untruth) 731
læge *nc* doctor, physician 658
lægge *v* to lay, put, place 746
lækker *adj* delicious 908
længe *adv* long 222
lære *v* to teach, learn 414
lærer *nc* teacher 655
lært *v* taught 718
lærte *v* taught 783
læse *v* to read 568
læst *nc* read 769
løbe *v* to run 345
løgn *nc* lie (untruth) 717
løj *v* lied, told untruth 969
løjtnant *nc* lieutenant 736
løs *adj* loose 723
lå *v* lay 853
låne *v* to borrow, lend 982

mad *nc* food 378
magt *nc* force, power 720
major *nc* major (rank) 975
makker *nc* partner, pal 570
man *pro* one, you, people 87
mand *nc* man 100
mange *adj* many, a lot 139
mangle *v* to lack 567
masse *nc* a lot, lots 461
med *prep* with 17
medicin *nc* medicine 967
medmindre *adv* unless 812
meget *adv* very, much 76
mellem *prep* between 399
men *conj* but 37
mene *v* to mean 142
mening *nc* meaning 498
menneske *nn* person 259
mens *conj* while 351
mente *v* meant 561
mere *adj* more 104
mest *adj* most 381
mester *nc* champion 608
meter *nc* meter 624
middag *nc* noon, dinner 687
midt *nc* middle 738
mig *pro* me 16
million *num* million 493
min *pro* my 42
minde *nn* a memory 835
mindre *adj* less 419
mindst *adv* least, at least 541
minut *nn* minute 868
minutter *nn* minutes 264
miste *v* to lose 739
mistede *v* lost 704
mistet *v* lost 597
mod *prep* towards, against 164
modtage *v* to receive 927
mor *nc* mother 126
mord *nn* murder 662
morder *nc* murderer 860
morgen *nc* morning 209

morges *adv* (this) morning 936
mulighed *nc* opportunity, possibility 813
muligt *adj* possible 468
mund *nc* mouth 659
musik *nc* music 734
myrde *v* to murder 922
mænd *nc* men 243
mærke *nn* mark, brand 544
møde *nn* meeting 280
møde *v* to meet 281
mødt *v* met 653
mødte *v* met 683
mørk *adj* dark 943
må *v* can, may, must 56
måde *nc* method, way 228
mål *nn* aim, goal, target 770
måned *nc* month 459
måske *adv* perhaps, maybe 97
måtte *v* have to, had to 425
nat *nc* night 396
naturligvis *adv* of course 689
navn *nn* name 205
ned *prep* down 123
nede *adv* down 448
nej *int* no 43
nem *adj* easy 776
nemlig *adv* namely, in fact 664
nervøs *adj* nervous 843
netop *adv* just, exactly 639
ni *num* nine 674
nogen *pro* some, any 96
nogensinde *adv* ever 313
noget *pro* some (neut) 44
nogle *pro* some (plural) 140
nok *adv* enough 86
normalt *adv* normally 669
nu *adv* now 39
nummer *nn* number 385
ny *adj* new 261
nyheder *nc* news (plural) 771
nær *adj* near, close 710
nærhed *nc* closeness 902

nærmere *adj* nearer, closer 988
næste *adj* next 239
næsten *adv* nearly, almost 319
nød *v* enjoyed 550
nødt *adj* need 221
nødvendigt *nc* necessary 855
nå *v* to reach, manage 183
når *conj* when 91
ofte *adv* often, frequently 999
og *conj* and 10
også *adv* too, as well, also 109
om *prep* about 38
omkring *adj* about, around 352
område *nn* area, space 862
ond *adj* bad, evil 347
onde *nn* evil 743
onkel *nc* uncle 574
op *prep* up 65
opgave *nc* task 741
oppe *adv* up 456
optaget *adj* occupied, busy 976
ord *nn* word 325
orden *nc* neatness, order 271
ordne *v* to order, arrange 673
ordre *nc* order (command) 667
os *pro* us 52
otte *num* eight 573
ovenpå *adv* on (the) top 929
over *prep* above 94
overalt *adv* everywhere 782
overfor *adv* opposite 920
overhovedet *adv* at all 630
overleve *v* to survive 879
overraskelse *nc* surprise 939
ovre *adj* over 898
par *nn* pair, couple 232
parat *adj* ready, prepared 735
pas *nn* passport 274
passe *v* to look after 412
penge *npl* money 208
perfekt *adj* perfect 463
person *nc* person 543
personlig *adj* personal 830

sindssyg *adj* insane, crazy 867
situation *nc* situation 903
sjov *adj* fun 365
sjæl *nc* soul 787
skabe *v* to create 944
skade *nc* damage, harm 586
skal *v* will (future) 35
skam *nc* shame, pity 752
skat *nc* tax, treasure 952
ske *v* to happen, occur 192
skib *nn* ship, boat 677
skid *nc* (vulgar) shit, damn 694
skifte *nn* to change 934
sko *nc* shoe 774
skole *nc* school 614
skrev *v* wrote 684
skrevet *v* written 719
skridt *nn* step, footstep 986
skrive *v* to write 538
skudt *v* shot 551
skulle *v* must, have to 99
skyde *v* to shoot 495
skylder *v* to owe 293
skynde *v* to hurry 432
skæbne *nc* destiny, fate 790
skød *v* shot 564
skør *adj* insane, crazy 682
slag *nn* blow, battle 950
slags *nc* kind, sort, type 288
slap *adj* let go, release 355
slem *adj* bad, serious 691
slet *part* at all 395
slippe *v* to drop 451
slog *v* hit (past tense) 442
slukke *v* to put out 921
slut *adj* over, finished 433
slå *v* to hit, beat 265
slået *v* beaten 592
slås *v* to fight 656
smerte *nc* pain, suffering 906
smuk *adj* beautiful 435
smule *nc* little bit 562
små *adj* small, little (plural) 418

snakke *v* to talk, speak 332
snart *adv* soon 238
soldat *nc* soldier 874
solen *nc* the Sun 892
som *pro* who (relative) 40
sort *adj* black 589
sove *v* to sleep 530
spil *nn* game 487
spille *v* to play 415
spise *v* to eat 405
spurgte *v* asked 638
spændende *adj* exciting 978
spørge *v* to ask, inquire 438
spørgsmål *nn* question 329
stadig *adj* constant, steady 154
stakkels *adj* poor, pitiful 833
stand *nc* position, rank 692
start *nc* start 857
starte *v* to start up, to start 709
sted *nn* place, spot 133
stemme *nc* voice 690
sten *nc* stone 804
stikker *nc* informer, snitch 932
stil *nc* style, manner 643
stille *adj* still, quiet, calm 258
stjal *v* stole 751
stjæle *v* to steal 886
stjålet *v* stolen 880
stod *v* stood 535
stol *nc* chair 766
stole *v* to rely on (stole på) 635
stolt *adj* proud 657
stoppe *v* to stop 219
stor *adj* large, great 225
straks *adv* at once 536
stykke *nn* piece 476
styre *nn* management 916
styre *v* to control, manage 917
styrke *v* to strengthen 756
stærk *adj* strong 707
større *adj* larger, bigger 576
største *adj* largest 540
stå *v* to stand 218

umuligt *adj* impossible 618
under *prep* under, below 204
underlig *adv* odd, strange 722
undgå *v* to evade, avoid 973
undskyld *int* sorry 125
undskylde *v* to apologize 712
ung *adj* young 445
utroligt *adv* incredibly 552
vagt *nc* guard, watch 889
valg *nn* election, choice 453
valgte *v* chose 907
vand *nn* water 408
vandt *v* won 851
var *v* was 32
varm *adj* warm, hot 871
ved *v* know 36
vegne *npl* behalf 974
vej *nc* road, way 158
vejr *nn* weather 569
vel *int* isn't it? 182
velkommen *int* welcome 349
ven *nc* friend 194
vende *v* to turn 646
venlig *adj* friendly 625
venstre *adj* left (direction) 482
vente *v* to wait 150
verden *nc* world 223
vi *pro* we 12
vide *v* to know 190
videre *adv* further, farther 341
vidste *v* knew 201
vigtig *adj* important 479
vil *v* want to, shall, will 31
vild *adj* wild 582
vilje *nc* will (volition) 895
ville *v* to want to, will 61
vinde *v* to win 522
vindue *nn* window 948

virke *v* to seem, appear 321
virkelig *adj* real, actual 149
vise *v* to show 350
vist *adv* shown 263
viste *v* showed 786
vor *pro* (formal) our, ours 801
vores *pro* our 93
vred *adj* angry 728
væk *adv* gone, away 127
vælge *v* to choose 864
vælger *nc* voter 996
værd *adj* worth 517
være *v* to be 47
værelse *nn* room 499
været *v* been 129
værre *adj* worse 525
værsgo *int* here you are 440
våben *nn* weapon 368
vågne *v* to wake up 821
ægte *adj* true, right 671
ældre *adj* older 971
ændre *v* to change 663
ære *nc* honor 601
ære *v* to honor 602
ærlig *adj* honest, sincere 826
ø *nc* island 968
ødelagt *adj* destroyed 796
ødelægge *v* to destroy 676
øje *nn* eye 430
øjeblik *nn* moment 241
øjne *nn* eyes 413
øl *nn* beer 729
ønske *v* to wish 286
ønske *nn* wish 488
åben *adj* open 621
åbne *v* to open 583
år *nn* year 137

Made in the USA
Middletown, DE
21 November 2020

24765806R00076